I0438923

Distribution and Condition of Young-of-Year Lost River and Shortnose Suckers in the Williamson River Delta Restoration Project and Upper Klamath Lake, Oregon, 2008–10—Final Report

By Summer M. Burdick and David A. Hewitt

Prepared in cooperation with The Nature Conservancy and the Bureau of Reclamation

Open-File Report 2012-1098

U.S. Department of the Interior
U.S. Geological Survey

U.S. Department of the Interior
KEN SALAZAR, Secretary

U.S. Geological Survey
Marcia K. McNutt, Director

U.S. Geological Survey, Reston, Virginia: 2012

For more information on the USGS—the Federal source for science about the Earth, its
natural and living resources, natural hazards, and the environment, visit *http://www.usgs.gov*
or call 1-888-ASK-USGS.

For an overview of USGS information products, including maps, imagery, and publications,
visit *http://www.usgs.gov/pubprod*

To order this and other USGS information products, visit *http://store.usgs.gov*

Contents

Figures

Tables

Conversion Factors, Datums, and Abbreviations and Acronyms

Conversion Factors

Multiply	By	To obtain
Length		
millimeter (mm)	0.03937	inch (in)
meter (m)	3.281	feet (ft)
kilometer (km)	0.6214	mile (mi)
Speed		
meters per second (m/s)	2.23	miles per hour (mph)
meters per second (m/s)	3.28	feet per second (fps)
Area		
hectares (ha)	2.471	acres (ac)

Temperature in degrees Celsius (°C) may be converted to degrees Fahrenheit (°F) as follows:
$$°F = (1.8 \times °C) + 32.$$

Datums

Horizontal coordinate information is referenced to the North American Datum of 1983 (NAD 83). Vertical datum is referenced to the BOR datum (NAVD 88-2.17ft.)

Abbreviations and Acronyms

Abbreviations	Meaning
DO	dissolved oxygen
LRS	Lost River sucker
NL	notochord length
OSU	Oregon State University
pH	potential hydrogen
SD	standard deviation
SNS	shortnose sucker
SNS-KLS	shortnose or Klamath largescale sucker
TNC	The Nature Conservancy
USGS	U.S. Geological Survey

Distribution and Condition of Young-of-Year Lost River and Shortnose Suckers in the Williamson River Delta Restoration Project and Upper Klamath Lake, Oregon, 2008–10—Final Report

By Summer M. Burdick and David A. Hewitt

Executive Summary

The Nature Conservancy undertook restoration of the Williamson River Delta Preserve with a primary goal "to restore and maintain the diversity of habitats that are essential to the endangered [Lost River sucker (*Deltistes luxatus*) and shortnose sucker (*Chasmistes brevirostris*)] while, at the same time, minimizing disturbance and adverse impacts" (David Evans and Associates, 2005). The Western Fisheries Research Center of the U.S. Geological Survey was asked by the Bureau of Reclamation to assist The Nature Conservancy in assessing the use of the restoration by larval and juvenile suckers. We identified five obtainable objectives to gauge the habitat suitability for young-of-year suckers in the permanently flooded portions of the two most recently restored sections (Goose Bay and Tulana) of the Williamson River Delta Preserve (hereafter referred to as the Preserve) and its effects on the distribution and health of larval and juvenile suckers. Several of these objectives were met through collaborations with The Nature Conservancy, Oregon State University, Oregon Water Science Center, and Leetown Science Center.

Our findings were in concurrence with those of The Nature Conservancy, who found that the Preserve supported young-of-year suckers at least as well as adjacent lake habitats (Erdman and others, 2011) despite the prevalence of non-native and piscivorous species in the system. The Preserve was recolonized by all fishes in the regional species pool, both native and non-native, between the time each portion of the Preserve (Goose Bay and Tulana) was inundated in autumn and the following spring. A large number of fish capable of preying on endangered larval suckers and a few fish that could prey on juvenile suckers were captured in the Preserve, but these species were no more abundant in the Preserve than in adjacent lakes.

Larvae and age-0, age-1, and age-2 juvenile Lost River and shortnose suckers were captured in the Preserve, Upper Klamath Lake, and Agency Lake, indicating that these species reared in restored and unaltered lake habitats. We captured too few larval suckers to examine patterns in spatial or temporal distribution. Once endangered suckers transitioned into juveniles, as defined by morphological development, they continued to disperse from shallow to deep water throughout the Preserve and into adjacent lakes. Age-1 and age-2 suckers captured throughout the Preserve and in adjacent lake habitats, especially in spring, show continued use of restored habitat by these species.

Quantitative examination of habitat use by age-0 juvenile suckers that accounted for imperfect detection indicated the portion of habitat used increased throughout July and August each year until the entire study area was used by one or more age-0 juvenile suckers by the end of August. Our rigorous evaluation showed both restored Preserve and unaltered lake habitats were equally used by age-0 juvenile suckers. Although all sampled habitats were used, multi-state occupancy models indicated that more age-0 suckers occupied shallow rather than deep habitats within the range of depths we sampled (0.5–4.3 m).

We were unable to compare health and condition of juvenile suckers among habitats, due to their movement among habitats. However, documentation of length-weight relationships, afflictions and deformities, and histology indicated juvenile suckers captured in all habitats maintained a similar level of health among the 3 years of our study.

Introduction and Background

Lost River sucker (*Deltistes luxatus*; LRS) and shortnose sucker (*Chasmistes brevirostris*; SNS) were listed as federally endangered in 1988 following apparent decreases in adult abundance (U.S. Fish and Wildlife Service, 1988). Although once abundant throughout their range, sucker populations were extirpated from Lower Klamath Lake, Sheepy Lake, and Lake of the Woods, and it is suspected that populations in Tule Lake and Keno Reservoir no longer reproduce (National Research Council, 2004). The primary threat to Lost River and shortnose sucker persistence is a lack of recruitment to the adult spawning populations (Janney and others, 2008; Hewitt and others, 2011), the cause of which is currently unknown, but could be attributed to poor water quality, avian predation, lack of suitable habitat, algal toxins, or some other factor.

The Williamson and Sprague Rivers provide one of two spawning habitats for LRS and SNS residing in Upper Klamath Lake, the other being lakeshore spring sites along the eastern boundary of the lake (National Research Council, 2004). Spawning for both species typically occurs between March and May (Ellsworth and others, 2009). Eggs are spread over gravel and cobble substrates (Andreasen, 1975). Between mid-April and late May, larvae spawned in the river systems emerge from gravel and drift downstream (Ellsworth and others, 2009). Larvae begin to reach the Preserve by late April (Crandall and others, 2008; Ellsworth and others, 2009). By mid-July, most young-of-year suckers have developed into juveniles (Kelso and Rutherford, 1996; U.S. Geological Survey, unpub. data, 2010). Between June and September, age-0 larval and juvenile suckers disperse throughout Upper Klamath Lake and its littoral marshes (Burdick and others, 2009b). Population demography, distribution, and habitat use during the transition from juvenile to adult life stages (a period of time between 5 and 7 years) is poorly understood (Burdick and others, 2009b).

Wind-driven water currents in Upper Klamath Lake typically flow in a clockwise direction and may push larvae originating from the Williamson and Sprague Rivers south along the eastern shore to the lake outlet and into Keno Reservoir (fig. 1). It is suspected that larvae entering Keno Reservoir are lost to the population due to poor survival and an inability to return to natal spawning locations (Markle and others, 2009). Markle and others (2009) estimate that prior to the restoration of the Preserve it took an average of 5 days for LRS and 10 days for SNS to be transported from the mouth of the Williamson River out of Upper Klamath Lake. The difference in transport time appears to be a function of when and where larvae drift in relation to the major lake currents (Markle and others, 2009). One hypothesized method for slowing the transport of larvae from the lake is to create well-vegetated marshes that allow fish to escape the main current (Markle and others, 2009).

Poor survivorship between juvenile and adult life stages is one of several reasons cited for the decrease and lack of recovery of LRS and SNS (National Research Council, 2004). Sharp decreases in age-0 catch rates during August and early September and extremely low catches of age-1 suckers indicate juvenile survival is the primary factor limiting recruitment into adult spawning populations (Simon and Markle, 2002; Hendrixson and others, 2007; Burdick and Brown, 2010). Poor juvenile survival may result from increased predation due to inadequate shelter from predators, any number of physiological stressors (for example, disease, toxins, or water quality), or some heretofore unrecognized age-class specific factor, all of which may be exacerbated by a lack of high quality rearing habitat.

Historically, larval and juvenile suckers had access to habitat in vast wetlands along the northern parts of Upper Klamath Lake and in the Preserve, which may have functioned as nurseries. Extensive diking and draining of wetlands for agriculture between 1915 and 1995 eliminated an estimated 66 percent of wetlands adjacent to Upper Klamath (Larson and Brush, 2010). Recent research indicates that age-0 juveniles use various habitats throughout Upper Klamath Lake, including stands of emergent vegetation in and around the Preserve (Burdick and others, 2009a). Age-1 suckers are concentrated near patches of vegetation in tributary mouths and springs during April and May (Markle and Simon, 1993; Burdick and Brown, 2010) and are found throughout Upper Klamath Lake in June and July (Bottcher and Burdick, 2010).

The Preserve likely was an important wetland for larval and juvenile suckers, due to its location downstream of known productive spawning grounds in the Williamson and Sprague Rivers (fig. 1) (National Research Council, 2004). Established wetlands composed of emergent macrophytes, similar to what probably historically existed in the Preserve, support more, larger, and better-fed larvae than habitats characterized as having submergent macrophytes, woody vegetation, or open water (Cooperman and Markle, 2004). More recently, larval suckers were documented in Riverbend and South Marsh, two pilot restoration wetlands at the Preserve, and in Tulana and Goose Bay (fig. 2) (Crandall and others, 2008; Hendrixson, 2008; Erdman and others, 2011). Historically, juvenile suckers may have reared for several months to several years in the emergent or submerged vegetation and deep water wetlands along marsh edges or in the marsh interior (National Research Council, 2004). Without the availability of the Preserve, larval suckers originating in the Williamson and Sprague Rivers could out-migrate into Upper Klamath Lake as rapidly as 1 day, often before caudal fin development occurs. Such rapid migration could reduce swimming performance and foraging success of larval suckers (Cooperman and Markle, 2000; 2003).

The Nature Conservancy (TNC) began restoring the Williamson River Delta in 1999, because this area is essential to the survival of the endangered suckers (David Evans and Associates, 2005). Restoration activities include breaching levees along Agency Lake and Upper Klamath Lake shorelines, filling toe drains, excavating and reconnecting an historical oxbow, creating an additional channel at the Williamson River mouth, creating a riparian bench and breaching levees along the Williamson River, and managing vegetation (David Evans and Associates, 2005). Hydrologic connectivity was achieved for more than 1,000 ha to the northwest of the Williamson River (Tulana) in October 2007 and an additional 1,000 or more ha to the southeast of the river in November 2008 (Goose Bay) (Erdman and others, 2011).

Prior to restoration, larval sucker monitoring occurred in the Williamson and Sprague Rivers (Ellsworth and others, 2009), Upper Klamath Lake (Simon and others, 2009), Riverbend and South Marsh restoration sites, and the shoreline of Goose Bay (Crandall and others, 2008; Erdman and others, 2011). In addition, juvenile sucker monitoring occurred throughout Upper Klamath Lake (Burdick and others, 2009b), and along the shore of Agency Lake (Simon and others, 2009). The U.S. Geological Survey (USGS) began work under contract with the Bureau of Reclamation (Interagency Agreement 07AA200135) to assist TNC in assessing the success of the delta restoration in providing high quality habitat for larval and juvenile fish in the permanently flooded areas of the project. The Nature Conservancy expanded their larval sampling program into the newly restored Tulana and Goose Bay areas of the Preserve (Erdman and Hendrixson, 2010; Erdman and others, 2011), and Oregon State University (OSU) adjusted their shoreline sampling to include the new contours of the lake shore (Simon and others, 2009). U.S. Geological Survey larval sampling differed from TNC's in the depth sampled and gear used, but our objectives with regard to understanding larval sucker use of restored habitat were similar. Collaboration between TNC, OSU, and USGS's Oregon Water Science and Western Fisheries Research Centers also was formed in 2008 to evaluate the effects of hydraulics and larval sucker behavior on larval distribution and retention in the Preserve (T. Wood, U.S. Geological Survey, written commun., 2011; Wood and others, 2011).

The specific objectives addressed in this report are:

- **Objective 1:** Describe geographic and temporal use of permanently flooded environments in the Preserve by larval and juvenile suckers.
- **Objective 2:** Compare the probability of habitat use by juvenile suckers among habitats in the Preserve and open-water areas of Upper Klamath and Agency Lakes.
- **Objective 3:** Compare fish species composition, with special attention to non-native and piscivorous fishes, in the Preserve, Upper Klamath Lake, and Agency Lake.
- **Objective 4**: Describe the temporal and spatial colonization of environments within the Preserve by juvenile suckers and other fish species.
- **Objective 5:** Compare the growth, condition, and health of juvenile suckers from the Preserve to those from Upper Klamath and Agency Lakes.

The rationale for each objective, methods used, and results are discussed below. A complete list of products produced with assistance from funding secured under Interagency Agreement 07AA200135 is given in appendix A.

Description of Study Area

The study area is located in south-central Oregon and includes the parts of the Preserve that were most recently restored (Tulana and Goose Bay), a southern part of Agency Lake, and a northern part of Upper Klamath Lake (fig. 1). The Williamson River is the largest tributary of Upper Klamath Lake. It flows approximately 85 km from its headwaters in Klamath Marsh and has one major tributary, the Sprague River. The Preserve connects Agency and Upper Klamath Lakes and is divided in two by the Williamson River: (1) Goose Bay to the south and east and (2) Tulana to the west and north (fig. 2). The lakes and permanently flooded wetland areas in Tulana are hypereutrophic and experience massive seasonal blooms of the cyanobacterium *Aphanizomenon flos-aquae*. These blooms are associated with dissolved oxygen (DO) concentrations that fluctuate between supersaturation and anoxia and pH levels that frequently exceed 9.0 (Lindenberg and others, 2008; Wong and others, 2010). High pH and low DO concentrations occur every summer at levels potentially lethal to juvenile LRS and SNS in Upper Klamath Lake and in the Preserve. High un-ionized ammonia concentrations also occasionally occur in Upper Klamath Lake (Wood and others, 2006).

There are six distinct habitats in the study area, based on the combination of location and type of plant community—three are located in Tulana, one in Goose Bay, one in southern Agency Lake , and one in northern Upper Klamath Lake (figs. 1 and 2). The Nature Conservancy defined wetland habitats in Tulana and Goose Bay based on the predicted response of broad-scale plant community types to hydrologic reconnection with the lakes and river following restoration (David Evans and Associates, 2005). Tulana habitats include: (1) the western part of Tulana predicted to remain unvegetated (Tulana Open Water), (2) an area located in the center of Tulana predicted to establish submergent vegetation (Tulana Submergent), and (3) the eastern side of Tulana predicted to establish emergent vegetation (Tulana Emergent; fig. 2). Tulana Submergent in our report is referred to as deep water wetland by TNC. The Agency Lake habitat includes a narrow waterway connecting Agency and Upper Klamath Lakes known as Agency Strait.

There is substantial variation in water depth and the abundance of aquatic vegetation, but very little variation in substrate composition among habitats. Substrate in the Preserve consists primarily of mud and clay (Lather muck and Tulana silt loam; David Evans and Associates, 2005), but substrates composed of sand mixed with gravel and cobble exist along the levy breaches. Agency and Upper Klamath Lakes are shallow (about 2–3 m) and mostly devoid of vegetation except along the shoreline. Agency Strait had a maximum depth of 7.4 m. Goose Bay has a maximum depth of about 1.2 m, but large portions of this area can be as shallow as 0.1 m or be completely dry by the end of September. This area is vegetated with patches of submergent and emergent vegetation (Elseroad and others, 2009). Tulana Open Water is the deepest and least vegetated of the areas in Tulana. Intermediate depths were found in Tulana Submergent (about 1.50–2.75 m deep during our sampling season), which was vegetated with scattered patches of submergent vegetation. Tulana Emergent was the shallowest area sampled in Tulana (< 1 m) and vegetation in this area was nearly all emergent macrophytes interspersed between patches of open water. On the eastern edge of Tulana Emergent, some riparian vegetation also occurred (Elseroad and others, 2009).

Larval Fish Collection

Larval fish distribution at a coarse habitat scale was assessed with plankton nets and random stratified sampling. Random sampling complemented fixed-site sampling that was designed to assess larval fish distribution along hydrologic pathways (T. Wood, U.S. Geological Survey, written commun., 2011). We randomly selected sites from three Tulana habitats, Upper Klamath Lake, and Agency Lake in 2008 and 2009 (fig. 2). We collected 1–3 samples at 8–12 randomly selected sites weekly between the beginning of May and early July in each of these years. Effort was equally divided among these habitats.

Plankton nets were used to collect larvae from the top of the water column. These nets had 0.3-m-diameter mouth openings, a 2.5-m-long tail, 800-μm-mesh Nitex netting, and a removable cod end. A General Oceanics™ model 2030R mechanical flow meter was mounted in the mouth of each net so that the volume sampled could be calculated. The net was towed parallel to a boat at approximately 1 m/s for 3–5 minutes or until algae began to clog the mesh. After retrieval, all material was removed from nets and samples were immediately preserved in 70–95 percent ethanol. We also recorded water temperature, water depth, and the portion of the sampled area covered by vegetation.

We collected three sequential tows at a subset of 18 percent of sites in 2008, 19 percent of sites in 2009, and at all sites in 2010 to assess sampling efficiency and the variability in catch rates. These replicate tows were all started at the site origin, but the direction of the tow varied slightly so that the same volume of water was not sampled in each replicate. Larval sucker catch rates were highly variable among replicates, indicating larvae are not uniformly distributed. Sample densities did not decrease in sequential larval samples, indicating replicate net tows did not deplete larvae at each site. Sample variability is described in detail in Burdick and others (2009a), Burdick and Brown (2010), and Burdick (2012).

In the laboratory, fish were identified to species or lowest taxonomic unit practical. Larval fish were identified based on gut length, body shape, and pigmentation (Remple and Markle, 2005; D. Simon, Oregon State University, written commun., 2004). Using this method, larval suckers were identified as Lost River suckers, or a group of either shortnose or Klamath largescale suckers (SNS-KLS). Sculpin (*Cottus* spp.) were identified to genus due to the lack of a suitable larval identification key for these species. The notochord lengths (NL) of the first 10 larvae of each non-sucker species and all larval suckers were measured and all larval fish were enumerated. Notochord and standard length are the same for larval suckers; therefore, this measurement is comparable to those reported by TNC and OSU. Larval density for each species was calculated by dividing the total number of fish in each sample by the volume of water filtered.

Juvenile Fish Collection

We used trap nets and a random stratified sampling approach to compare juvenile fish distribution and condition among habitats in the Preserve, northern Upper Klamath Lake, and southern Agency Lake. Trap nets were rectangular with mouth dimensions of 0.61 × 0.91 m, a 10-m-lead, and three internal fykes. Nets were set overnight for a target soak time of about 20 hours and water depth was recorded at each net site. In 2008, sites were randomly chosen from three habitats in Tulana, and one each in southern Agency Lake and northern Upper Klamath Lake (fig. 2). Sample sites were added in Goose Bay in 2009 after this area was flooded in fall 2008. In 2010, a reduced budget forced us to alternate weeks in which Agency and Upper Klamath Lakes were sampled. We also refined our habitat stratification in northern Upper Klamath Lake and southern Agency Lake in 2010 by redefining these areas in terms of four habitats: Fish Banks, Mid-North, Agency Strait, and Agency Near Shore (fig. 3). Sample allocation was initially distributed equally among habitats within each year, but as the shallowest habitats became inaccessible due to declining lake-surface elevation, effort was reallocated to deep areas. Low lake-surface elevations prevented us from sampling in the shallow Goose Bay or Tulana Emergent habitats after July 23, 2008, August 25, 2009, and July 19, 2010.

Lake habitats were defined based on a combination of location, depth, and nearness to vegetation. Fish Banks was less than 1.5-m-deep and vegetated with emergent macrophytes. Mid-North and southern Agency Lake habitats were approximately 1 to 2.5-m deep and mostly unvegetated. Water depth in Agency Strait was up to 5 m deep, but due to the narrow shape of this habitat unit no site within it was more than 20 m from emergent vegetation. Overall, water depth at our sample sites ranged from 0.5 to 4.3 m, and 96 percent of samples were collected in water less than 4 m deep.

Data collection within a subset of sampling weeks each year was designed to meet the requirements for occupancy analyses that allow for quantitative estimation of detection and habitat-use probabilities for rare species, such as suckers. Repeat samples, which may occur over space or time, are necessary to estimate the probability of habitat use when detection is imperfect or variable. Repeat sampling was conducted between June 23 and July 28 in 2008, June 30 and August 31 in 2009, and August 2 and September 13, 2010.

Our strategy for obtaining repeat samples for use in occupancy models changed between the 2009 and 2010 field seasons, following initial data analysis and reevaluation of our methods. We obtained repeat samples at sites by setting multiple trap nets simultaneously in 2008 and 2009, allowing us to estimate changes in habitat use as a function of time. Evaluation of this technique in 2009 revealed that use of trap nets and spatial replication may lead to a negative bias in habitat use, especially at times of the year when the abundance of juvenile suckers is low (Burdick and Hewitt, U.S. Geological Survey, unpub. data, 2009). Therefore, in 2010 we redesigned our sampling such that repeat samples were obtained by setting a single trap net at a site three times within a week. Replicate samples were collected at a large number of sites on one occasion in 2008 and one occasion in 2009, whereas replicate samples were collected at a small number of sites every 2 weeks in 2010. Our 2010 sampling reduced bias in estimates of habitat use and still allowed for evaluation of habitat use over time, albeit over a 2 week rather than a 1 week period.

We recorded the condition and standard length (SL) of all suckers, and length and abundance data were collected on non-target species from all nets set in 2008 and 2009, and about 10 percent of nets set in 2010. Parasites, deformities, emaciation, red marks, or unusual appearances were noted. Approximately one-third of all suckers shorter than 70 mm SL, and one-tenth of all suckers 70–140 mm SL were sacrificed and preserved in 95-percent denatured ethanol for later identification and a concurrent histology study. Suckers were sacrificed throughout the week in 2008 and 2009, but were only sacrificed on the last day of sampling each week in 2010. In the laboratory, we weighed each sacrificed sucker and identified juvenile suckers to the species level following Markle and others (2005) using a combination of techniques that included vertebrae enumeration, lip morphology, and gill-raker counts. We classified suckers as age-0, age-1, or older based on weekly length frequency plots. Otoliths and fin rays were examined from approximately 10 suckers collected in 2008 and 2009 to confirm age classification.

Catch per unit effort for each species and age class was calculated as fish per net rather than fish per hour because there was no evidence of a relation between the number of hours nets soaked and the number of fish captured. To estimate the number of suckers of each species, the composition of sacrificed suckers from each habitat and week was applied to the unsacrificed portion of suckers caught in each net.

Recolonization of the Williamson River Delta by Juvenile and Small Adult Fishes

Understanding the recolonization process in the Preserve will help in developing expectations for future wetland restoration projects in and around Upper Klamath Lake, and may help to identify potential interactions among species. Wetlands can recover a maximum number of species after years of desiccation in as little as a few months (Paller, 1997; Baber and others, 2002), or as long as 5 years (Simenstad and Thom, 1996). We predicted the Preserve would be quickly recolonized by all fishes common to Upper Klamath and Agency Lakes, given connectivity to these habitats.

In initial post-restoration trap-net sampling, species richness, unadjusted for detection probability, was similar in restored habitats and adjacent lakes (table 1). Furthermore, richness in restored habitats did not change substantially in subsequent sampling, indicating recolonization by all species occurred within 6–7 months after flooding the Preserve. Of the 14 species detected throughout the study area, at least 10 were detected in every habitat every year: largemouth bass (*Micropterus salmoides*), Klamath redband trout (*Oncorhynchus mykiss newberrii*), slender sculpin (*Cottus tenuis*), and Klamath speckled dace (*Rhinichthys osculus klamathensis*) were not detected in all habitats. Absences of these species from our sampling in some habitats and in some years probably is due to a low probability of detection and should not be interpreted as true absence from habitats. Rapid recolonization of restored habitats is probably the result of the location of the Preserve relative to source populations, the high level of connectivity between the Preserve and source populations, and suitability of restored habitats for these fishes.

Description of the Fish Assemblage and Evaluation of the Risk of Predation to Endangered Suckers

We used species composition to describe habitat use by juvenile and small adult fishes in the study area and the risk of predation to larval and juvenile suckers. The number and relative abundance of native and non-native fish species were used to describe fish assemblages. We summarize catches and distribution of piscivorous fishes, because a large number of these species have the potential to reduce the overall benefits of the restoration to suckers, especially if they co-occur with suckers small enough to be preyed upon. A fish species is considered to be a potential larval sucker predator if it is known to eat larval fish and a potential juvenile sucker predator if it is known to eat fish of similar size to the juvenile suckers captured in this study. Diets were determined based on a literature review and not directly verified. We assumed that Klamath tui chub (*Siphatales bicolor bicolor*) eat larval fish based on the finding by Bond and others (1968) and that blue chub (*Gila coerulea*) collected concurrently in Upper Klamath Lake ate larval fish and appeared to have similar diets to Klamath tui chub. This assumption is also loosely supported by an observation by Koch (1973) that tui chub eat cui-ui sucker (*Chasmistes cujus*) eggs in the Truckee River. Although we believe it is reasonable to assume that tui chub prey on larval suckers, Klamath tui chub diets should be confirmed. The only species captured in this study for which there is specific documentation of predation on suckers is fathead minnow. Fathead minnow (*Pimephales promelas*) ate larval suckers in a laboratory study in which the larval suckers were the only prey item (Markle and Dunsmoor, 2007). The diets for each species are given in table 2.

The juvenile and small adult fish assemblage was similar in the Preserve, adjacent lakes, and in the Upper Klamath National Wildlife Refuge marsh (Mulligan and Mulligan, 2007), indicating restored habitat was no more or less suitable than unaltered habitat. Five non-native and eight piscivorous fishes were captured. Potential larval sucker predators (table 2) far outnumbered non-predators in all habitats, but were proportionally more abundant in our samples in the Tulana Open Water and Tulana Submergent habitats in 2008 and 2009 and in the Tulana Emergent habitat in 2010 (table 3). Potential juvenile sucker predators were outnumbered by fish that could not prey on juvenile suckers in all habitats and in all years (table 4). Non-native fish outnumbered native fish in most habitats and years (table 5). Native fishes were more abundant than non-native fishes in Tulana Emergent and northern Upper Klamath Lake in 2008 and 2010, in southern Agency Lake in 2008, and in Goose Bay in 2010 (table 5).

Based on their relative abundance and co-occurrence with larval suckers, non-native adult fathead minnow and native juvenile Klamath tui chub have the potential to consume more larval suckers than other predatory fishes. During the time period in which larval suckers were present each year, these two species made up 53 percent of trap-net catches in 2008, 90 percent in 2009, and 80 percent in 2010. Non-native yellow perch (*Perca flavescens*) and native blue chub also were present during these time periods but made up substantially smaller portions of the catch. Fathead minnows and Klamath tui chubs were at least as abundant in our trap-net catches in the habitats most used by larval suckers (Tulana Emergent and Goose Bay) as they were in other habitats during the time period that larval suckers were detected. Relatively large catches of fathead minnows in May and June occurred about as frequently in Tulana Emergent and Goose Bay as they did in all other habitats, with the exception of northern Upper Klamath Lake where large catches were less common. Klamath tui chub, on the other hand, were slightly more abundant in 2009 and 2010 May and June samples in the Tulana Emergent habitat than in other habitats.

Yellow perch per trap net frequently numbered in the hundreds, but few were large enough to prey on juvenile suckers. Using the length- and gape-size limitations of yellow perch (Truemper and Lauer, 2005), we determined that 0.6 percent in 2008, 16 percent in 2009, and 4 percent in 2010 could prey on the smallest age-1 suckers. Twenty-three percent of yellow perch in 2008 and 2009 and 10 percent in 2010 could prey on the smallest age-0 suckers concurrently present (fig. 4). Yellow perch large enough to prey on juvenile suckers were found in all habitats sampled and we did not detect a pattern in their relative abundance among habitats.

Detection of the larvae of four piscivorous fishes—fathead minnow, yellow perch, blue chub, and tui chub—indicated that the areas sampled provided some rearing habitat for these species. Yellow perch larvae were rare in our trawls and in larval sampling conducted by TNC (Erdman and Hendrixson, 2010, 2011), indicating that this species primarily spawns outside of our study area or is difficult to detect until the juvenile life stage. Catches of the other three species were much more common throughout the study area, indicating these species rear in the Preserve and in the lakes.

Geographic and Temporal Use of the Restored Williamson River Delta by Larval and Juvenile Suckers

Two primary goals of the Williamson River Delta restoration project are to retain and provide quality rearing habitat for larval Lost River and shortnose suckers. Retention of sucker larvae in wetland habitats may play a role in good year-class formation (Markle and others, 2009) by providing high quality juvenile sucker rearing habitat that may in turn assist suckers in surviving to recruitment. We examined larval catch data to determine if larval suckers were retained in restored habitats in the Preserve. In addition, we compared catch data in both restored Preserve habitats and unaltered lake habitats to determine when and where juvenile suckers reared.

Fewer than 25 larvae of either sucker taxa were captured within a single sampling season in any sampling area, with the exception of Lost River sucker larvae captured in Upper Klamath Lake near the mouth of the Williamson in 2008 (n=82) and SNS-KLS larvae captured in Tulana Emergent in 2009 (n= 84). Therefore, catch data had to be pooled across either space or time for comparisons to be made, and any conclusions drawn from these data are tentative.

Larval Sucker Distribution Among Habitats

Both larval sucker taxa were most frequently detected in 2008 and 2009 random stratified sampling in the Tulana Emergent, compared to the Tulana Open Water, Upper Klamath Lake, or Agency Lake (table 6). Once flooded, Goose Bay became accessible to larval suckers and opened a new pathway for entry into Upper Klamath Lake. Larval-transport modeling indicated larvae are distributed with the aid of wind-driven water circulation and prevailing spring winds from the northwest pushed larval suckers into Goose Bay in 2009 (T. Wood, U.S. Geological Survey, written commun., 2011). We were unable to detect this pattern with our sampling in 2008 and 2009 because we did not sample in Goose Bay (fig. 5).

Lost River sucker larvae were captured at higher rates than SNS-KLS larvae in all habitats in 2008, whereas SNS-KLS larvae were captured at higher rates than Lost River larvae in all habitats except Tulana Open Water in 2009 where only Lost River suckers were captured (table 7; fig. 6). This pattern was inconsistent with the pattern in species dominance for larval drift sampled in the Williamson River; SNS-KLS were more prevalent than Lost River suckers in 2008 and the opposite was true in 2009 (Ellsworth and others, 2011; Ellsworth and Martin, 2012). Larval sucker catch rates in the Williamson River were approximately 100 times greater than catch rates in our study area, and are a better indication of species composition in each year. Not only were our catches sparse they were unevenly distributed. For example, 82 of 114 Lost River sucker larvae captured in 2008 were captured in a single sample.

Our inability to detect consistent patterns in species composition contrasts with TNC's consistently higher SNS-KLS catches compared to LRS catches. Ratios of larval Lost River to SNS-KLS captured in TNC pop nets set in water less than approximately 1-m-deep in Tulana and Goose Bay were 0.22 in 2008, 0.10 in 2009, and 0.12 in 2010 (Erdman and Hendrixson, 2010, 2011). The inferences that can be made from TNC catches may be more reliable, given that they captured 5 to 10 times more larvae over the same time period that we sampled. Differential habitat use by these two taxa as larvae probably is due to a combination of behavior (for example, rheotaxis or habitat selection) and drift timing relative to hydrodynamics (T. Wood, U.S. Geological Survey, written commun., 2011). Due to their apparent habitat preferences, SNS-KLS larvae might have benefited more than LRS larvae from restoration due to the increase in shallow vegetated habitat that is otherwise in relatively low abundance in Upper Klamath and Agency Lakes, but both species probably benefited somewhat from the restoration.

Temporal Use of the Williamson River Delta by Larval Suckers

Due to very low larval catch rates, our ability to assess the timing of larval sucker habitat use is extremely limited. Lost River suckers were captured in relatively high abundance in this study at the mouth of the Williamson River between May 22 and June 10, 2008, and SNS-KLS were captured in relatively high numbers between May 26 and May 31, 2009.

Studies conducted concurrently with this study indicated sucker larvae used Goose Bay beginning in May and Tulana Emergent beginning in early June (Burdick and others, 2009a; Burdick and Brown, 2010; Erdman and Hendrixson, 2010, 2011; Burdick, 2012). Catches of larval suckers in fixed site plankton tows that were collected for the validation of larval transport models corroborated general timing observed in the study described in this report; a large pulse of Lost River sucker larvae were captured at the mouth of the Williamson River between May 20 and May 27, 2008 (Burdick and others, 2009a), and relatively high numbers of SNS-KLS were captured in Tulana Emergent between May 18 and June 8, 2009 (Burdick and Brown, 2010). These data also indicated a relatively high concentration of SNS-KLS used Tulana Emergent between June 24 and June 30, 2008, despite the fact they were not detected in high abundance in the random stratified sampling described in this report (Burdick and others, 2009a). Finally, fixed-site plankton sampling indicated that both larval sucker taxa were detected in relatively high abundance in Goose Bay in May and were detected in Tulana Emergent after a wind-reversal event in early June 2009 and 2010 (Burdick and Brown, 2010; Burdick, 2012). Relatively high catches of SNS-KLS larvae captured in pop nets set in shallow water (< 1 m) primarily occurred in the first 2 weeks of June in 2009 and 2010 in both Tulana Emergent and Goose Bay (Erdman and Hendrixson, 2010, 2011). Because pop nets catch more large larval suckers (10–27 mm; Erdman and Hendrixson, 2011) than surface-oriented plankton trawls (10–19 mm, captured in our study), peak concentrations of SNS-KLS larvae in Goose Bay in early to mid-June as witnessed by Erdman and Hendrixson (2010) and Erdman and others (2011) rather than throughout May, as we observed, may indicate fish were retained and grew in that habitat.

Timing and Distribution of Age-0 Juvenile Sucker Catches

The spatial differentiation in habitat use between larval sucker taxa did not carry over into the juvenile life stage. Our age-0 sucker catches were composed of more shortnose than Lost River suckers in Tulana Open Water and Tulana Submergent habitats in all 3 years, and in Goose Bay in 2009 and 2010. Ratios of these species, however, varied among years in other habitats sampled (table 8). Age-0 suckers appeared to be ubiquitously distributed throughout the study area and catch rates did not show consistent differences among habitats (fig. 7; table 9). Differential habitat use among species at the juvenile life stage likely is driven by a number of interacting factors, including different larval distributions and habitat preferences.

Throughout most of the study area, age-0 suckers primarily were captured in August and early September in 2008, 2009, and 2010 (fig. 8). Exceptions occurred in the shallow Tulana Emergent habitat where most age-0 suckers were captured in mid-July in 2008, in early August in 2009, and not at all in 2010. Another exception was in Goose Bay where age-0 suckers were only captured on July 19 in 2010. The initiation of catches each year depends on age-0 suckers reaching a size that can be retained by the mesh size of our nets, whereas the decrease in catches is due to mortality, emigration from sampling areas, or both. Small numbers of age-0 suckers in Goose Bay and no age-0 suckers in Tulana Emergent in 2010 indicate suckers did not recruit to our gear before these areas became too shallow to sample after July 19.

Timing and Distribution of Age-1 and Older Juvenile Sucker Catches

The timing of age-1 sucker catches was similar among years within habitats, but catch rates for age-1 suckers were lower in 2010 than in the previous 2 years (table 10). Age-1 suckers primarily were captured between early May and early July in 2008, 2009, and 2010 (fig. 9). Catches of this age class occurred slightly earlier in the shallow Goose Bay and Tulana Emergent habitat when compared to the other four deeper habitats, an observation that may be confounded by our inability to effectively sample these shallow water habitats as lake-surface elevation declined each year (Burdick and others, 2009a; Burdick and Brown, 2010; Burdick, 2012). In all 3 years of this study, weekly catches of age-1 suckers decreased to zero or near zero by early September. The initiation of age-1 sucker catches each year roughly coincided with the start of sampling, whereas the decrease in catches probably is a result of mortality, emigration from the study area, reduced selectivity of this age class, or a combination of these factors.

Catches of age-1, age-2, and older juveniles were too sparse in all 3 years of the study to imply patterns in their distribution among habitats. Our data did not indicate a spatial pattern in the species ratio for age-1 endangered suckers, nor did they indicate distributional patterns within habitats for either species (fig. 7). Three juvenile suckers in 2008, two in 2009, and nine in 2010 captured in our trap nets were judged to be age-2 or older based on weekly length-frequency plots. These captures occurred in both lakes and in all three Tulana habitats between May and September (Burdick and others, 2009a; Burdick and Brown, 2010; Burdick, 2012).

Quantitative Comparisons of Habitat Use by Age-0 Juvenile Suckers

Juvenile suckers use various habitats throughout Upper Klamath Lake, including areas near-shore and off-shore, in vegetated and open waters, and over a number of different substrates (Terwilliger and others, 2004; Hendrixson and others, 2007; Burdick and others, 2009b). Therefore, it was predicted that juvenile suckers would use open water, unvegetated habitats, deep water wetlands, and emergent vegetation habitats throughout the Preserve. It was not clear, however, if juvenile suckers would use restored and previously established habitat equally. Occupancy approaches allowed for quantitative estimates of the portion of restored habitat used by juvenile suckers and a method to compare these estimates among various habitats in the Preserve and between restored (for example, Goose Bay and Tulana) and established (Upper Klamath and Agency Lakes) habitats throughout the lake. In 2008 and 2009, we used single-state occupancy models (MacKenzie and others, 2006) to evaluate the effect of depth and habitat (figs. 1 and 2) on the probability of habitat use. A change in sample design in 2010 allowed us to use the extended multi-state version of an occupancy model, with states based on relative abundance (MacKenzie and others, 2006). We also redefined our habitat stratification within northern Upper Klamath Lake and southern Agency Lake in 2010 by redefining these areas in terms of four habitats: Fish Banks, Mid-North, Agency Strait and Agency Near Shore (fig. 3). Therefore, 2010 data required a separate analysis from 2008 and 2009 data.

Quantitative Estimation of Sucker Habitat Use

To estimate the portion of habitat used by age-0 juvenile suckers, we used an occupancy modeling approach (MacKenzie and others, 2006). This approach uses repeat sampling to estimate the probability that any one site is used given imperfect detection. In its most general form, an occupancy model (MacKenzie and others, 2002) describes the probability of detecting the species of interest y times out of k occasions at site i. Modeling is based on encounter histories that summarize the samples at each site (for example, 010 indicates that at least one sucker was captured in the second sample but none were captured in the other two samples). The model is used to jointly estimate the probability of a site being occupied by the species of interest (ψ) and the probability of detecting the species given that it occupies the site (p). We did not attempt to generate estimates of habitat use for Goose Bay in 2008 because it was dry.

Several assumptions are necessary for occupancy models to yield unbiased estimates. First, the presence of the species of interest and the ability to detect that species when it is present are assumed independent between repeated samples at a site. Second, site-specific local populations that are susceptible to the sampling gear are assumed to be closed to changes in habitat use in the case of single state models used in 2008 and 2009 and in their state of abundance (few or many) in the case of multi-state models used in 2010. Because our sampling was designed to detect changes in occupancy over time, it is important that sites are closed to these changes within but not among weeks. Violation of this closure assumption can result in biased estimates of occupancy (MacKenzie and others, 2006; Rota and others, 2009). This assumption can be relaxed if violations occur randomly among sites, but the resulting probability estimates are of habitat use rather than occupancy (MacKenzie and others, 2006). It also is necessary to assume that the species of interest is never falsely detected. Species misidentification would violate this assumption; therefore, we were unable to model habitat use for the two sucker species separately.

Models, which were mathematical descriptions of working hypotheses to explain juvenile sucker distributions among habitats and water depth, were constructed in program R (R Development Core Team, 2010) and passed to program MARK (version 6.0; White and Burnham, 1999) using the RMark package (Laake and Rexstad, 2009; Laake, 2010). Models in each model set were ranked using Akaike's Information Criterion adjusted for small sample size (AICc; Burnham and Anderson, 2002) to determine which model in each suite of models was most parsimonious given the data. Normalized weights (w_i) were calculated for each model. Normalized model weights can be interpreted as the probability that a particular model is the best one in the set for explaining the data, and were used to estimate model-averaged estimates of ψ (Burnham and Anderson, 2002).

Quantitative Estimates of the Portion of Habitat Used by Age-0 Suckers

Model selection indicated that habitat use differed among weeks and the areas sampled in 2008 and 2009. There was some model selection uncertainty among the four most parsimonious models in 2008, all of which included an additive effect of habitat and week on habitat use (table 11). The uncertainty among these models is due to minor effects on detection probability. Given very small increases in AICc values with additional parameters, we conclude that effects of covariates on p in 2008 were minimal. Model selection was much more certain in 2009 with nearly all of the weight being assigned to a single model that included an effect of water depth on p and an additive effect of habitat and week on ψ (table 12). None of the models with a covariate for water depth on ψ carried any weight in either 2008 or 2009 (tables 11 and 12), but almost all of our sample sites were in water less than 4 m deep.

Models indicated that habitat use increased during July in 2008 and 2009. In 2008, the portion of used habitat increased between June 23 and July 28 when replicate samples were collected. We stopped collecting replicate samples suitable for occupancy analysis at the end of July in 2008; however, and were unable to determine if the portion of used habitat continued to increase after that time. By the end of July 2008, more than 30 percent of Tulana Submergent and northern Upper Klamath Lake, 50 percent of Tulana Open Water, and 80 percent of Tulana Emergent and Agency Lake habitats were in use by age-0 juvenile suckers (fig. 10). Because catch per unit effort increased in all habitats during August, we assume that habitat use also continued to increase but we are unable to determine the maximum portion of habitat used. In 2009, all sampled areas were being used by age-0 suckers by the end of August. The probability of habitat use as a function of week reached an asymptote of one in the first week of August in 2009 in Goose Bay and by late August in all other habitats (fig. 10). Because no data were collected in Tulana Emergent or Goose Bay in late August, model parameter estimates for those habitats in that time period are based on the data from other habitats. As a result, lines shown in figure 10 may not accurately represent age-0 sucker use of Tulana Emergent and Goose Bay habitats in late August.

Quantitative Estimation of Habitat Use by Low and High Abundances of Age-0 Suckers

In 2010, we used a multi-state occupancy model (MacKenzie and others, 2006). In this scheme, each sample at a site was classified as low (1–5) or high (>5) abundance of suckers, with the threshold at 5 based on a natural break in the data. Thus, encounter histories provide information about the variability in state classification based on the repeated samples at the site (for example, 0HL indicates that suckers were not captured in sample 1, more than five suckers were captured in sample 2, and one to five suckers were captured in sample 3).

For comparison of habitat use among habitats within each week we developed a list of 16 *a priori* candidate models to describe each dataset (table 13). In cases where the probability of ψ_{low} was estimated to be 1 or had estimated standard errors overlapping the upper estimation limit of 1 (that is, suckers were present nearly everywhere) in all of the top five models, we fixed it at one and eliminated models with covariates for ψ_{low}, reducing the total number of models in the set to four. We estimated detection probabilities (p) of high or low abundances of suckers and the probability of incorrectly classifying the state of abundance without the addition of covariates. We used model averaging over the confidence set of models to estimate probabilities of habitat use by a low (1–5; ψ_{low}) or high (>5; ψ_{high}) abundance of age-0 suckers in each week. The confidence set of models was defined as the best models in the set that had normalized model weights $\left(w_i\right)$ summing to no less than 0.9. We were unable to estimate habitat use in Goose Bay or Tulana Emergent in 2010 because these areas became too shallow to sample just 1 week after age-0 suckers recruited to our nets.

To examine the effect of depth on the probability of the presence of a high abundance of age-0 suckers across all weeks and areas, we fit a single model to a pooled dataset. For this model, we assumed that suckers existed in low abundance in all areas and all weeks, based on the results from the separate weekly models. We fixed ψ_{low} at one and modeled ψ_{high} as a function of depth. We report the relationship between sampling depth and the probability that more than five age-0 suckers used a site.

Quantitative Estimates of Habitat Use by Abundance Classes of Age-0 Suckers

Model selection consistently indicated age-0 suckers were ubiquitous among sampled habitats in 2010, but abundance varied among habitats and depths in some weeks. The top-ranked models for each week carried the large majority of the model weights between the weeks of August 9–15 and August 30–September 5 and during the week of September 13-19, but there was more model selection uncertainty during the other weeks (table 14). The parameter ψ_{low} was fixed at 1 between the weeks starting August 9 and August 23 and during the week of September 13–19. Variation in ψ_{high} was explained by the categorical habitat covariate during the weeks of August 9–15 to August 23–29 and by depth during the weeks of August 2–8, August 23–29, and August 30–September 5.

The probability that at least one age-0 sucker was present at a given site (ψ_{low}) was similar among habitats within each week, except the week of August 2–8. During the week of August 2–8, sites within the Mid-North and Tulana Submergent habitats had a lower probability of being used by one or more age-0 suckers than sites in the Tulana Open Water and Fish Banks habitats (table 15). During all other weeks in all habitats the probability of a site being occupied by one or more age-0 suckers was at least 0.83. One-half of ψ_{low} estimates were equal to the upper estimation limit of 1 and nearly all other estimates had confidence intervals that reached 1.

These high estimates of ψ_{low} are consistent with the high estimated portion of habitat used in 2008 and 2009.

Multi-state occupancy models indicated a relatively large portion of habitats were occupied by a high abundance (> 5) of age-0 suckers between the weeks of August 16–22 and August 23–29, whereas few habitats were occupied by a high abundance during the weeks of August 30–September 5 and September 6–12 (table 16). Model selection uncertainty (table 14) and large standard errors on estimates during most weeks (table 16) indicate that our ability to detect a pattern in habitat use by high abundances of age-0 suckers was limited because catches of more than five age-0 suckers were too infrequent.

Multi-state occupancy modeling indicated that depth did not influence habitat use much by a low abundance of age-0 suckers, but high abundances of age-0 suckers occurred more often in shallow water than deep water in 2010. To model the effect of depth on habitat use by more than five age-0 juvenile suckers, we pooled data over the entire 2010 sampling season and all habitats. The portion of habitat used by more than five age-0 suckers decreased only slightly with depths between 0.5 and 4.3 m (fig. 12). Previously, researchers indicated that age-0 suckers were less likely to use deep water (0.5 m or deeper) (Buettner and Scoppettone, 1990) than shallow water (Burdick and others, 2008). Our results indicate that suckers are likely to be present at all depths less than or equal to 4.3 m deep, but may be more abundant on the shallower end of this range.

Condition and Health of Juvenile Suckers

Understanding spatial differences in condition and health of juvenile suckers may elucidate the causes behind the continuing problem of poor recruitment, and help assess the value of habitats throughout Upper Klamath Lake, including the newly restored habitat in the Preserve. Poor water quality or other prolonged environmental factors may cause or exacerbate poor juvenile sucker health, which may eventually lead to mortality.

Afflictions that may be correlated with high rates of mortality in young suckers were identified throughout the study area during the first 3 years after restoration. Assessment of habitat effects on growth, condition, and health of juvenile suckers, however, was confounded by movement of juvenile suckers among habitats in our study area (Burdick and Brown 2010; Burdick, 2012). Sucker movement among habitats prevented us from associating fish condition at the time of capture to the habitat in which the fish was captured. Nonetheless, juvenile suckers captured in all habitats appeared to have similar levels of overall health among the 3 years of our study. We cannot make inferences about the condition of juvenile suckers relative to historical data because adequate baselines for comparison do not exist.

Skeletal deformities in juvenile suckers in our study are of concern, given their potential for lethal side effects, inconsistency with other fish species in the study area, and an increase from juvenile suckers collected in Upper Klamath Lake in the early 1990s. The most common deformity we observed was shortened opercula, but scoliosis and fused vertebrae also were observed in 2010. The portion of age-0 suckers in our study with shortened opercula was greater (≥ 6.7 percent; table 17) than what Plunkett and Snyder-Conn (2000) found in 1993 (4.7 percent of age-0 Lost River and 1.4–3.1 percent of age-0 shortnose suckers). This deformity was not noted for any other species captured in our study, but has been noted for bull trout *Salvelinus confluentus* (Smith and Tinniswood, 2008) and adult suckers (E. Janney, U.S. Geological Survey, oral commun., 2011) in the Upper Klamath Basin. Opercle deformities that expose gill filaments are a common phenomenon in hatchery fish but are less prevalent in wild fish (Beraldo and others, 2003). These deformities are non-lethal for hatchery-raised fish (Beraldo and others, 2003), but may lower resistance to oxygen stress and predispose fish to infections by bacteria, parasites, and fungi (Galeotti and others, 2000; Beraldo and others, 2003). Deformed opercula could be caused by inbreeding (Winemiller and Taylor, 1982; Tringali and others, 2003), a lack of dietary ascorbic acid (Chávez de Martínez, 1990), a lack of dietary calcium (Lindesjoo and others, 1994), pollution (Lindesjoo and others, 1994), low environmental pH during periods of rapid growth (Lindesjoo and others, 1994), or infestations of digenea (Quist and others, 2007). There are no data with which to assess the first three of these. Urban pollutants associated with deformities in other systems (Lindesjoo and others, 1994) are not known to be present in Upper Klamath Lake. In Upper Klamath Lake, daily summertime median pH is rarely less than 8.0 (Lindenberg and others, 2008), suggesting low pH is not the cause of the deformities we observed. We did not examine fish microscopically and therefore were unable to determine if deformities were associated with infestations of digenea. Whatever the causal factor, skeletal deformities are irreversible (Beraldo and others, 2003).

The presence of parasitic female anchorworms on juvenile suckers is noteworthy given their apparent absence prior to 1996 (Simon and others, 2009), but this parasite is unlikely to cause mortality in young suckers. Anchorworm intensity is not associated with deleterious health effects for suckers at intensities less than 30 per fish (Robinson and others, 1998). One juvenile sucker had an infestation of 34 anchorworms, but otherwise the maximum parasite intensity in our 3-year study was 24. Although direct mortality from anchorworms is unlikely, this parasite creates a wound at the point of attachment where a secondary infection may occur (Khalifa and Post, 1976).

We documented the length-weight relation of Lost River and shortnose suckers as a gross assessment of fish condition during each year of this study, and detected no meaningful differences in condition among years (fig. 13). Weight at length assessments, such as this one, are only useful in describing extreme changes in body condition. To better understand changes in health of juvenile suckers as they relate to restoration, the USGS generated a list of potential bacterial pathogens, examined histology, and evaluated the usefulness of TGF-beta protein production as an indicator of prolonged stress. A total of 304 bacterial genera was detected in skin mucous of age-0 juvenile suckers, several of which are potentially pathogenic (Burdick and others, 2009a). Further research is necessary to determine which bacteria pose a serious health risk to suckers. A high incidence of poor liver histology in juvenile suckers was coincident with high levels of the microcystin cyanotoxin (Vanderkooi and others, 2010), but further research is required to determine the nature of this relation. The quality of RNA used to quantify TGF-beta decreases with increased air temperatures that typically occur later in the sampling season, and decreased RNA quality negatively biases estimates of TGF-beta. Therefore, TGF-beta may be of little use in identifying temporal trends in juvenile sucker stress unless improved sampling methods are developed to address this issue (L. Robertson, U.S. Geological Survey, written commun., 2011).

Summary

The Williamson River Delta restoration project successfully recreated habitat for all fishes commonly found in Upper Klamath and Agency Lakes. Adverse effects of restoration on the fish community in general or on endangered suckers specifically were not detected. The quality of restored habitat was at least as suitable for rearing endangered suckers as adjacent lake habitats. Although a large number of non-native fishes and fish that could prey on larval suckers were captured in the Preserve, they were not more abundant in restored delta than unaltered lake habitats. The capture of several age classes of juvenile Lost River and shortnose suckers indicated these species used the restored habitat, at least seasonally, for up to 2 years. Quantitative habitat-use estimation that accounted for imperfect detection indicated that all restored habitat was used by age-0 juvenile suckers by the end of August each year, but more age-0 suckers used shallow rather than deep water.

Acknowledgments

Data were collected with the help of USGS staff Matt Abel, Caley Boone, Daniel Brown, Jared Bottcher, Ryan Braham, Travis Ciotti, Ernest Chen, Megan Dethloff, Nathan Harris, Terra Kemper, James Latshaw, Randal Loges, Nicholas Miller, Debra Wahrenbrock, Anna Willard and Jolene Willis. Greta Blackwood (USGS), Alta Harris (USGS) and Amari Dolan-Caret (USGS) helped with database development and management. Craig Ellsworth (USGS), Heather Hendrixson (TNC), Douglas Markle (Oregon State University), Torrey Tyler (USBR), Tamara Wood (USGS), and Scott VanderKooi (USGS) helped with study design. TNC allowed access to the land that much of this study was conducted on and provided us with bathymetry and vegetation map data used in this report to map the delta. This work was funded by the Bureau of Reclamation (Interagency Agreement 04AA204032) and the U.S. Geological Survey.

References Cited

Andreasen, J.K., 1975, Systematics and status of the family Catostomidae in southern Oregon: Corvallis, Oregon State University, Ph.D. thesis, 80 p.

Angradi, T.R., Spaulding, J.S., and Koch, E.D., 1991, Diel food utilization by the Virgin River spinedace, *Lepidomeda mollispinis mollispinis*, and speckled dace, *Rhinichthys osculus*, in Beaver Dam Wash, Utah: The Southwestern Naturalist, v. 36, p. 158–170.

Baber, M.J., Childers, D.L., Babbitt, K.J., and Anderson, D.H., 2002, Controls on fish distribution and abundance in temporary wetlands: Canadian Journal of Fisheries and Aquatic Science, v. 59, p. 1,441–1,450.

Beamish, R.J., 1980, Adult biology of the river lamprey (*Lampetra ayresi*) and Pacific lamprey (*Lampetra tridentata*) of the Pacific coast of Canada: Canadian Journal of Fisheries and Aquatic Sciences, v. 37, p. 1,906–1,923.

Beraldo, P., Pinosa, M., Tibaldi, E., and Canavese, B., 2003, Abnormalities of the operculum in gilthead sea bream (*Sparus aurata*)—morphological description: Aquaculture, v. 220, p. 89–99.

Bond, C.E., Hazel, C.R., and Vincent, D., 1968, Relations of nuisance algae to fishes in Upper Klamath Lake–Terminal Progress Report: U.S. Federal Water Pollution Control Administration, 126 p.

Bottcher, J., and Burdick, S.M., 2010, Temporal and spatial distribution of endangered juvenile Lost River and shortnose suckers in relation to environmental variables in Upper Klamath Lake, Oregon— 2009 annual data summary: U.S. Geological Survey Open-File Report 2010-1261, 42 p. (Also available at *http://pubs.usgs.gov/of/2010/1261/*.)

Burdick, S.M, 2012, Distribution and condition of larval and juvenile Lost River and shortnose suckers in the Williamson River Delta restoration project and Upper Klamath Lake, Oregon— 2010 annual data summary: U.S. Geological Survey Open-File Report 2012-1027, 39 p. (Also available at *http://pubs.usgs.gov/of/2012/1027/*.)

Burdick, S.M., and Brown, D.T., 2010, Distribution and condition of larval and juvenile Lost River and shortnose suckers in the Williamson River Delta restoration project and Upper Klamath Lake, Oregon—2009 annual data summary: U.S. Geological Survey Open-File Report 2010-1216, 78 p. (Also available at *http://pubs.usgs.gov/of/2010/1216/*.)

Burdick, S.M., Hendrixson, H.A., and VanderKooi, S.P., 2008, Age-0 Lost River and shortnose suckers nearshore habitat use in Upper Klamath Lake, Oregon—A patch occupancy approach: Transactions of the American Fisheries Society, v. 137, p. 417–430.

Burdick, S.M., Ottinger, C., Brown, D.T., VanderKooi, S.P., Robertson, L., and Iwanowicz, D., 2009a, Distribution, health, and development of larval and juvenile Lost River and shortnose suckers in the Williamson River Delta restoration project and Upper Klamath Lake, Oregon— 2008 annual data summary: U.S. Geological Survey Open-File Report 2009-1287, 76 p. (Also available at *http://pubs.usgs.gov/of/2009/1287/*.)

Burdick, S.M., VanderKooi, S.P., and Anderson, G.O., 2009b, Spring and summer spatial distribution of endangered juvenile Lost River and shortnose suckers in relation to environmental variables in Upper Klamath Lake, Oregon—2007 annual report: U.S. Geological Survey Open-File Report 2009-1043, 56 p. (Also available at *http://pubs.usgs.gov/of/2009/1043/*.)

Burnham, K.P., and Anderson, D.R., 2002, Model selection and multimodel inference: a practical information-theoretic approach (2nd ed.): New York, Springer, 496 p.

Buettner, M., and Scoppettone, G.G., 1990, Life history and status of Catostomids in Upper Klamath Lake, Oregon: Seattle National Fisheries Research Center, p. 119.

Cooperman, M.S., and Markle, D.F., 2000, Ecology of Upper Klamath Lake shortnose and Lost River suckers—Larval ecology of shortnose and Lost River suckers in the lower Williamson River and Upper Klamath Lake: Corvallis, Oregon State University, Department of Fisheries and Wildlife, 27 p.

Cooperman, M.S., and Markle, D.F., 2003, Rapid out-migration of Lost River and shortnose suckers from in-river spawning beds to in-lake rearing grounds: Transactions of the American Fisheries Society, v. 132, p. 1,138–1,153.

Cooperman, M.S., and Markle, D.F., 2004, Abundance, size, and feeding success of larval shortnose suckers and Lost River suckers from different habitats of the littoral zone of Upper Klamath Lake: Environmental Biology of Fishes, v. 71, p. 365–377.

Crandall, J.D, Bach, L.B., Rudd, N., Stern, M., and Barry, M., 2008, Response of larval Lost River and shortnose suckers to wetland restoration at the Williamson River Delta, Oregon: Transactions of the American Fisheries Society, v. 137, p. 402–416.

Chávez de Martínez, M.C., 1990, Vitamin C requirement of the Mexican native cichlid *Cichlasoma urophthalmus* (Gunther): Aquaculture, v. 86, p. 409–416.

David Evans and Associates, Inc., 2005, Williamson River Delta restoration environmental impact statement: Portland, Oregon, David Evans and Associates, Inc., 187 p.

Dibble, E.D., and Harrel, S.L., 1997, Largemouth bass diets in two aquatic plant communities: Journal of Aquatic Plant Management, v. 35, p. 74–78.

Elseroad, A., Aldous, A., Rudd, N., and Hendrixson, H., 2009, Williamson River Delta Preserve vegetation monitoring—Tulana first-year post-breaching results: The Nature Conservancy, 10 p.

Ellsworth, C.M., Banks, D.T, and VanderKooi, S.P., 2011, Patterns of larval sucker emigration from the Sprague and Lower Williamson Rivers of the Upper Klamath Basin, Oregon, prior to the removal of Chiloquin Dam—2007/2008 annual report: U.S. Geological Survey Open-File Report 2011-1108, 40 p. (Also available at http://pubs.usgs.gov/of/2011/1108/.)

Ellsworth, C.M., and Martin, B.A., 2012, Patterns of larval sucker emigration from the Sprague and Lower Williamson Rivers of the Upper Klamath Basin, Oregon, after the removal of Chiloquin Dam—2009–10 annual report: U.S. Geological Survey Open-File Report 2012-1037, 42 p. (Also available at http://pubs.usgs.gov/of/2012/1037/.)

Ellsworth, C.M., Tyler, T.J., VanderKooi, S.P., and Markle, D.F., 2009, Patterns of larval sucker emigration from the Sprague and Lower Williamson Rivers, Oregon, prior to the removal of Chiloquin Dam—2006 annual report: U.S. Geological Survey Open-File Report 2009-1027, 32 p. (Also available at http://pubs.usgs.gov/of/2009/1027/.)

Erdman, C.S., and Hendrixson, H.A., 2010, Larval shortnose and Lost River sucker response to large scale wetland restoration of the north half of the Williamson River Delta Preserve, Oregon—2009 annual data summary: The Nature Conservancy, 32 p.

Erdman, C.S., and Hendrixson, H.A., 2011, Larval Lost River and shortnose sucker response to large scale wetland restoration at the Williamson River Delta Preserve–2010 annual data summary: The Nature Conservancy, 28 p.

Erdman, C.S., Hendrixson, H.A., and Rudd, N.T., 2011, Larval sucker distribution and condition before and after large-scale restoration at the Williamson River Delta, Upper Klamath Lake, Oregon: Western North American Naturalist, v. 71, p. 472–480.

Galeotti, M., Beraldo, P., de Dominis, S., D'Angelo, L., Ballestrazzi, R., Musetti, R., Pizzoloito, S., and Pinosam, M., 2000, A preliminary histological and ultrastructural study of opercular anomalies in gilthead sea bream larvae (*Sparus aurata*): Fish Physiology and Biochemistry, v. 22, p.151–157.

Garcia-Berthou, E., and Moreno-Amich, R., 2000, Food of introduced pumpkinseed sunfish–ontogenetic diet shift and seasonal variation: Journal of Fish Biology, v. 57, p. 29–40.

Hendrixson, H.A., 2008, Non-native fish species and Lost River and shortnose suckers use of restoration and undisturbed wetlands at the Williamson River Delta—Final report of activities conducted in 2006 and 2007: Report of The Nature Conservancy to the U.S. Fish and Wildlife Service, Klamath Falls, Oregon, 28 p.

Hendrixson, H.A., Burdick, S.M., and VanderKooi, S.P., 2007, Near-shore and offshore habitat use by endangered, juvenile Lost River and shortnose suckers in Upper Klamath Lake, Oregon—Annual report 2004: Report of U.S. Geological Survey, Western Fisheries Research Center, Klamath Falls Field Station to Bureau of Reclamation, Mid-Pacific Region, Klamath Falls, Oregon, 94 p.

Hewitt, D.A., Hayes, B.S., Janney, E.C., Harris, A.C., Koller, J.P., and Johnson, M.A., 2011, Demographics and run timing of adult Lost River (*Deltistes luxatus*) and shortnose (*Chasmistes brevirostris*) suckers in Upper Klamath Lake, Oregon, 2009: U.S. Geological Survey Open-File Report 2011-1088, 38 p.

Janney, E.C., Shively, R.S., Hayes, B.S., Barry, P.M., and Perkins, D., 2008, Demographic analysis of Lost River sucker and shortnose sucker populations in Upper Klamath Lake, Oregon: Transactions of the American Fisheries Society, v. 137, p. 1,812–1,825.

Johnson, J.M., and Post, D.M., 1996, Morphological constraints on intracohort cannibalism in age-0 largemouth bass: Transactions of the American Fisheries Society, v. 125, p. 809–812.

Kelso, W.E., and Rutherford, D.A., 1996, Collection, preservation, and identification of fish eggs and larvae, *in* Murry, B.R., and Willis, D.W., eds., Fisheries techniques (2nd ed.): Bethesda, Maryland, American Fisheries Society, p. 255–302.

Khalifa, K.A., and Post, G., 1976, Histopathological effects of *Lernaea cyprinacea* (a copepod parasite) on fish: The Progressive Fish Culturist, v. 38, p. 110–113.

Kline, J.L., and Wood, B.M., 1996, Food habits and diet selectivity of the brown bullhead: Journal of Freshwater Ecology, v. 11, p. 145–151.

Koch, D.L., 1973, Reproductive characteristics of the Cui-ui lakesucker (*Chasmistes cujus Cope*) and its spawning behavior in Pyramid Lake, Nevada: Transactions of the American Fisheries Society, v. 102, p. 145–149.

Laake, J., 2010, RMark—R code for MARK analysis—Version 1.9.9: accessed April 20, 2012 at *www.phidot.org/software/mark/rmark*.

Laake, J., and Rexstad, E., 2009, RMark—An alternative approach to building linear models in MARK—Appendix C, *in* Cooch, E., and White, G., eds., Program MARK—A gentle introduction: accessed April 20, 2012 at *www.phidot.org/software/mark/docs/book*.

Larson, R., and Brush, B.J., 2010, Upper Klamath basin wetlands—An assessment: Klamath Falls, Oregon, U.S. Fish and Wildlife Service, 25 p.

Lindenberg, M.K., Hoilman, G., and Wood, T.M., 2008, Water-quality conditions in Upper Klamath and Agency Lakes, Oregon, 2006: U.S. Geological Survey Scientific Investigations Report 2008-5201, 23 p. (Also available at *http://pubs.usgs.gov/sir/2008/5201/.*)

Lindesjoo, E., Thulin, J., Bengtsson, B.E., and Tjärnlund, U., 1994, Abnormalities of a gill cover bone, the operculum, in perch *Perca fluviatilis* from a pulp mill effluent area: Aquatic Toxicology, v. 28, p. 189–207.

MacKenzie, D.L., Nichols, J.D., Lachman, G.B., Droege, S., Royle, J.A. and Langtimm, C.A., 2002, Estimating site occupancy rates when detection probabilities are less than one: Ecology, v. 83, p. 2,248–2,255.

MacKenzie, D.L., Nichols, J.D., Royle, J.A., Pollock, K.H., Bailey, L.L., and Hines, J.E., 2006, Occupancy estimation and modeling—Inferring patterns and dynamics of species occurrence: San Francisco, California, Elsevier Publishing, 344 p.

Markle, D.F., 2011, Size-structured spatial patterns as a measure of larval dispersal and emigration: Western North American Naturalist, v. 71, p. 456–471.

Markle, D.F., Cavalluzzi, M.R., and Simon, D.C., 2005, Morphology and taxonomy of Klamath Basin suckers (Catostomidae): Western North American Naturalist, v. 65, p. 473–489.

Markle, D.F., and Clauson, K., 2006, Ontogenetic and habitat-related changes in diet of late larval and early juvenile suckers (Catostomidae): Western North American Naturalist, v. 66, p. 492–501.

Markle, D.F., and Dunsmoor, L.K., 2007, Effects of habitat volume and fathead minnow introduction on larval survival of two endangered sucker species in Upper Klamath Lake, Oregon: Transactions of the American Fisheries Society, v. 136, p. 567–579.

Markle, D.F., Reithel, S.A., Crandall, J., Wood, T., Tyler, T., Terwilliger, M., and Simon, D.C., 2009, Larval fish transport and retention and the importance of location for juvenile fish recruitment in Upper Klamath Lake, Oregon: Transactions of the American Fisheries Society, v. 138, p. 328–347.

Markle, D.F., and Simon, D.C., 1993, Preliminary studies of systematics and juvenile ecology of Upper Klamath Lake Suckers—Final Report: Corvalis, Oregon State University.

Mulligan, T. J., and Mulligan, H.L., 2007, Habitat utilization and life history of fishes in Upper Klamath National Wildlife Refuge Marsh, Fourmile Creek and Odessa Creek, Oregon: Report of Humboldt State University to Bureau of Reclamation, Klamath Falls, Oregon, 278 p.

National Research Council, 2004, Endangered and threatened fishes in the Klamath River Basin—Causes of decline and strategies for recovery: Washington, D.C., The National Academies Press, 398 p.

Paller, M. H., 1997, Recovery of a reservoir fish community from drawdown related impacts: North American Journal of Fisheries Management, v. 17, p. 726–733.

Plunkett, S.R., and Snyder-Conn, E., 2000, Anomalies of larval and juvenile shortnose and Lost River suckers in Upper Klamath Lake, Oregon: U.S. Fish and Wildlife Service, Klamath Falls Fish and Wildlife Office, Klamath Falls, Oregon, 25 p.

Quist, M.C., Bower, M.R., and Hubert, W.A., 2007, Infections by black spot-causing species of Uvulifer and associated opercular alteration in fishes from a high-desert stream in Wyoming: Diseases of Aquatic Organisms, v. 78, p. 129–136.

R Development Core Team, 2010, R: a language and environment for statistical computing, R Foundation for Statistical Computing, Vienna, Austria, accessed April 30, 2012, at*www.R-project.org.*

Remple, S., and Markle, D.F., 2005, Description and identification of larval and juvenile cyprinids (fathead minnow, tui chub, and blue chub) from Upper Klamath Lake, Oregon: California Fish and Game, v. 91, no. 2, p. 83–99.

Robinson, A.T., Hines, P.P., Sorensen, J.A., and Bryan, S.D., 1998, Parasites and fish health in a desert stream and management implications for two endangered fishes: North American Journal of Fisheries Management, v. 18, p. 599–608.

Rota, C.T., Fletcher, Jr., R.J., Dorazio, R.M., and Betts, M.G., 2009, Occupancy estimation and the closure assumption: Journal of Applied Ecology, v. 46, p.1,173–1,181.

Simenstad, C.A., and Thom, R.M., 1996, Functional equivalency trajectories of the restored Gog-Le-Hi-Te estuarine wetland: Ecological Applications, v. 6, p. 38–56.

Simon, D.C., and Markle, D.F., 2002, Ecology of Upper Klamath Lake shortnose and Lost River suckers—Annual survey of abundance and distribution of age-0 shortnose and Lost River suckers in Upper Klamath Lake—2001 annual report: Report of Oregon Cooperative Research Unit, Department of Fisheries and Wildlife, Oregon State University to U.S. Biological Resources Division, U.S. Geological Survey, Corvallis, Oregon, and Klamath Project, Bureau of Reclamation, Klamath Falls, Oregon, 63 p.

Simon, D.C., Terwilliger, M.R., and Markle, D.F., 2009, Larval and juvenile sucker ecology of Upper Klamath Lake: Annual report for the Great Basin cooperative ecosystems study unit agency program USBR#2-FG-81-0813, Report of Oregon Cooperative Research Unit, Department of Fisheries and Wildlife, Oregon State University, U.S. Geological Survey, Corvallis, Oregon, submitted to Klamath Project, Bureau of Reclamation, Klamath Falls, Oregon, 179 p.

Smith, R., and Tinniswood, W., 2008, Draft bulltrout management direction, Threemile Creek, Klamath, County: Oregon Department of Fish and Wildlife, Klamath Falls, Oregon, 12 p.

Terwilliger, M.R., Simon, D.C., and Markle, D.F., 2004, Larval and juvenile ecology of Upper Klamath Lake suckers—1998–2003—Final report: Report of Oregon State University to Bureau of Reclamation, Klamath Falls, Oregon, 217 p.

Tringali, M.D., Ziemann, D.A., and Stuck, K.C., 2003, Preliminary aspects of genetic management for Pacific Threadfin *Polydactylus sexfilis* stock enhancement research in Hawaii *in* Nakamura, Y., McVey, J.P., Leber, K., Neidig, C., Fox, S., and Churchill, K., eds., Ecology of Aquaculture Species and Enhancement of Stocks—Proceedings of the Thirtieth U.S.–Japan Meeting on Aquaculture, Sarasota, Florida, December 3-4, 2001: UJNR Technical Report No. 30, Mote Marine Laboratory, p. 55–74.

Truemper, H.A., and Lauer, T.E., 2005, Gape limitation and piscine prey size-selection by yellow perch in the extreme southern area of Lake Michigan, with emphasis on two exotic prey items: Journal of Fish Biology, v. 66, p. 135–149.

U.S. Fish and Wildlife Service, 1988, Endangered and threatened wildlife and plants—Determination of endangered status for the shortnose sucker and Lost River sucker: Federal Register, v. 53 p. 27,130–27,134.

VanderKooi, S.P., Burdick, S.M., Echols, K.R., Ottinger, C.A., Rosen, B.H., and Wood, T.M., 2010, Algal toxins in Upper Klamath Lake, Oregon—Linking water quality to juvenile sucker health: U.S. Geological Survey Fact Sheet 2009-3111, 2 p. (Also available at http://pubs.usgs.gov/fs/2009/3111/.)

White, G.C., and Burnham K.P., 1999, Program MARK—Survival estimation from populations of marked animals: Bird study supplement, v. 46, p. 120–138.

Winemiller, K.O., and Taylor, D.H., 1982, Inbreeding depression in the convict cichlid, Cichlasoma nigrofasciatum (Baird and Girard): Journal of Fish Biology, v. 21, p. 399–402.

Wong, S., Hendrixson, H.A., and Doehring, C., 2010, Post-restoration water quality conditions at the Williamson River Delta, Upper Klamath Basin, Oregon, 2007–2009: The Nature Conservancy, Klamath Basin Field Office, Klamath Falls, Oregon, 70 p.

Wood, T.M., Hendrixson, H.A., Markle, D.F., Erdman, C.S., Burdick, S.M., Ellsworth, C.M., and Buccola, N.L., 2011, Dispersal of larval suckers at the Williamson River Delta, Upper Klamath Lake, Oregon, 2006–09: U.S. Geological Survey Scientific Investigations Report 2012-5016, 28 p. (Also available at *http://pubs.usgs.gov/sir/2012/5016/.*)

Wood, T.M., Hoilman, G.H., and Lindenberg, M.K., 2006, Water quality conditions in Upper Klamath Lake, Oregon, 2002–2004: U.S. Geological Survey Open-File Report 2006-5209, 64 p. (Also available at *http://pubs.usgs.gov/sir/2006/5209/.*)

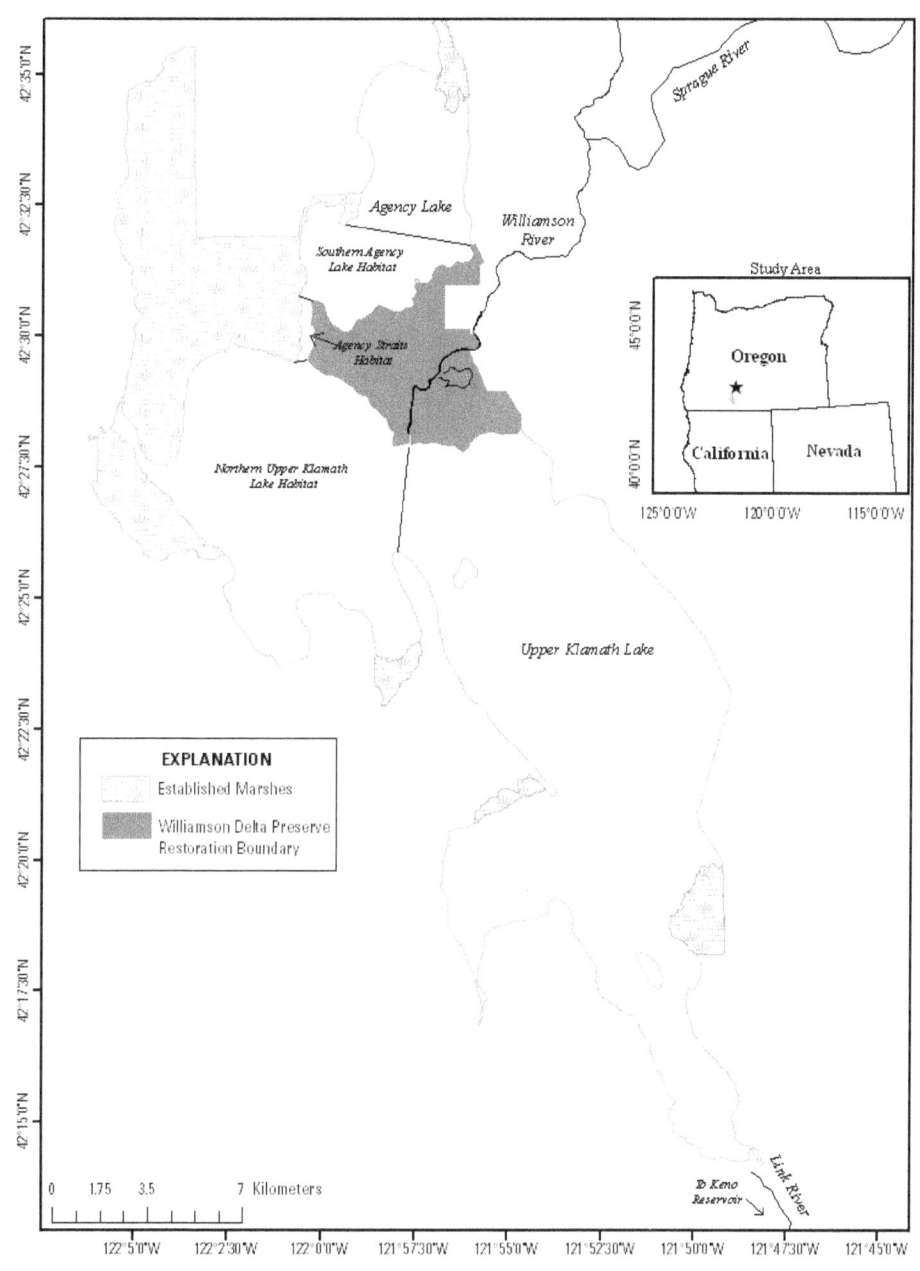

Figure 1. Geographic location of the Williamson River Delta Preserve Restoration Project in relation to other aquatic environments and state boundaries.

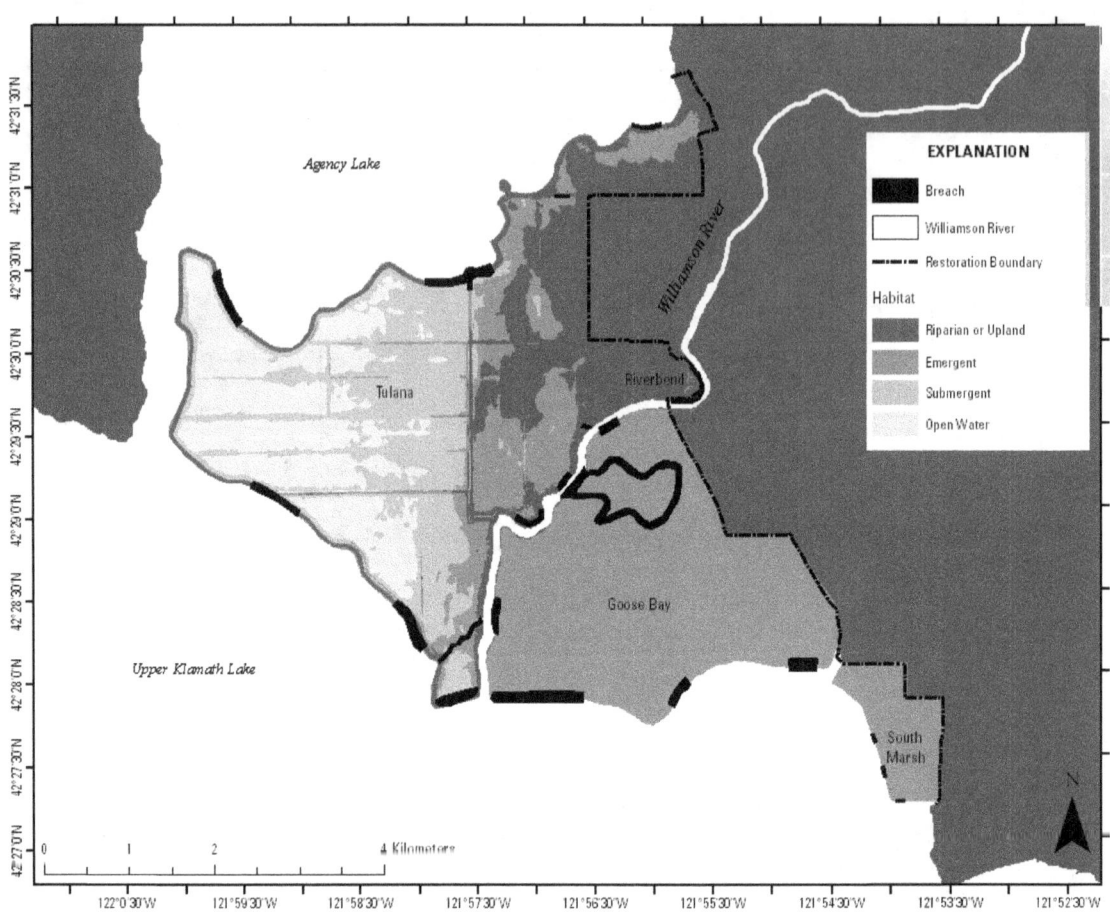

Figure 2. Habitats sampled in and adjacent to the Williamson River Delta, Oregon. Habitats within the Williamson River Delta were delineated based on vegetation types expected to occur following restoration. Goose Bay was sampled for juvenile fish using trap nets in 2009 and 2010; southern Agency Lake, northern Upper Klamath Lake, and Emergent, Submergent, and open water habitats in Tulana were sampled for juvenile fish from 2008 to 2010; southern Agency Lake, northern Upper Klamath Lake, and Emergent, and Open water habitats in Tulana for larval fish in 2008 and 2009.

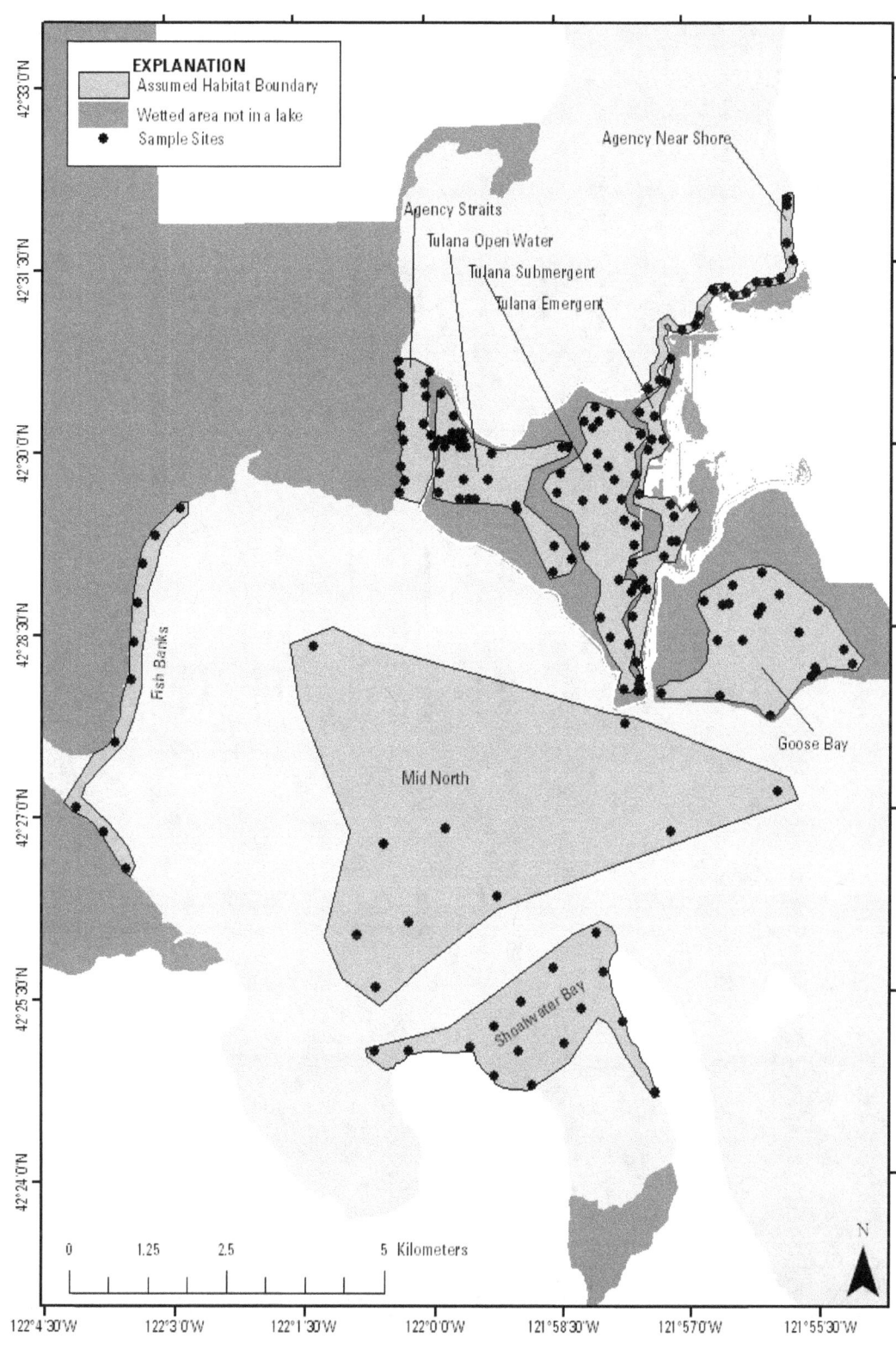

Figure 3. Locations of nine sampling areas and sites sampled with trap nets during summer 2010 in Upper Klamath Lake, Agency Lake, and the Williamson River Delta Preserve, Oregon.

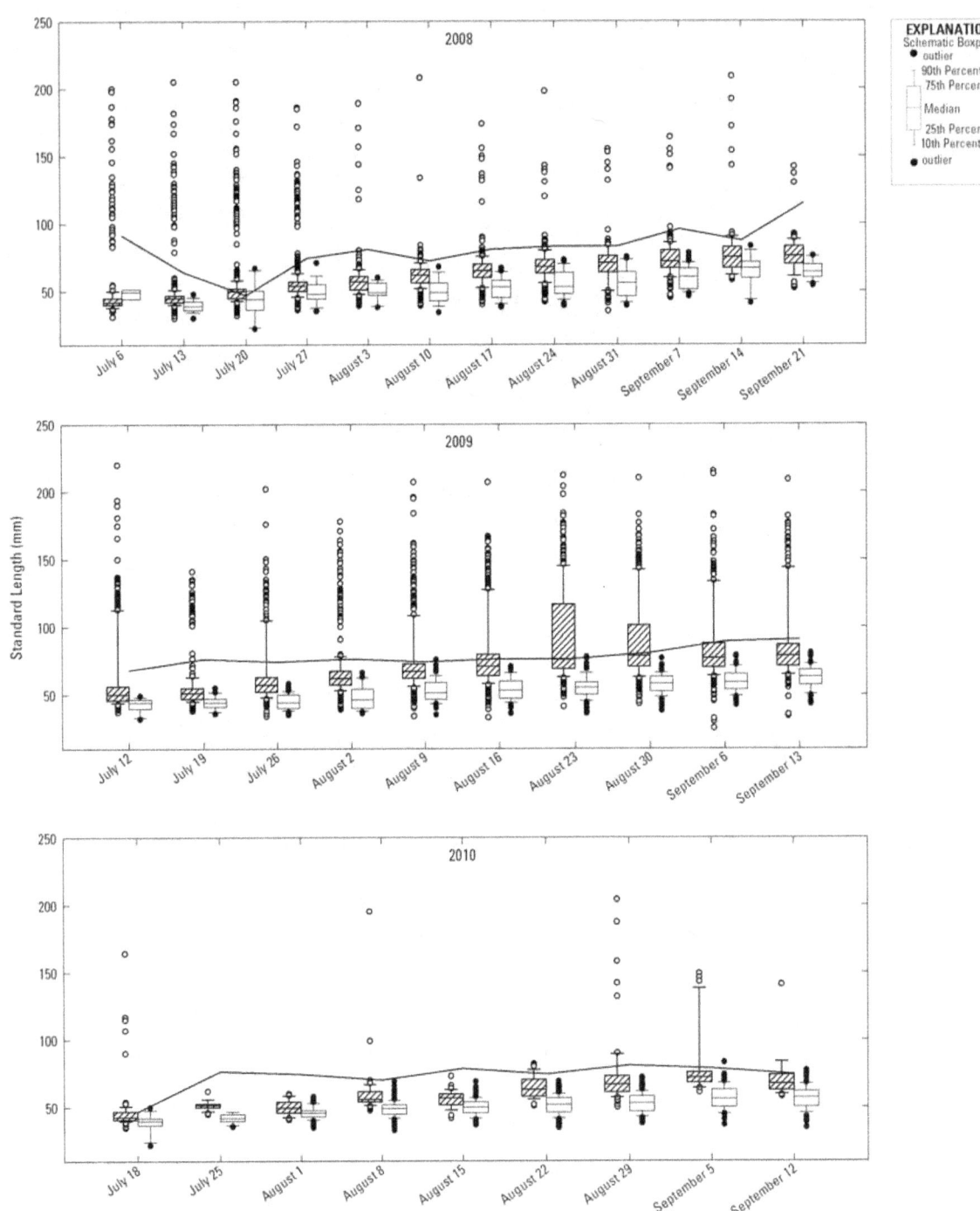

Figure 4. Schematic boxplots of standard length of yellow perch and age-0 juvenile suckers, captured in the Williamson River Delta, Oregon, and adjacent lake habitats, 2008–10. The line indicates the minimum size a yellow perch would need to be to prey on the smallest age-0 sucker captured in trap nets in a given week.

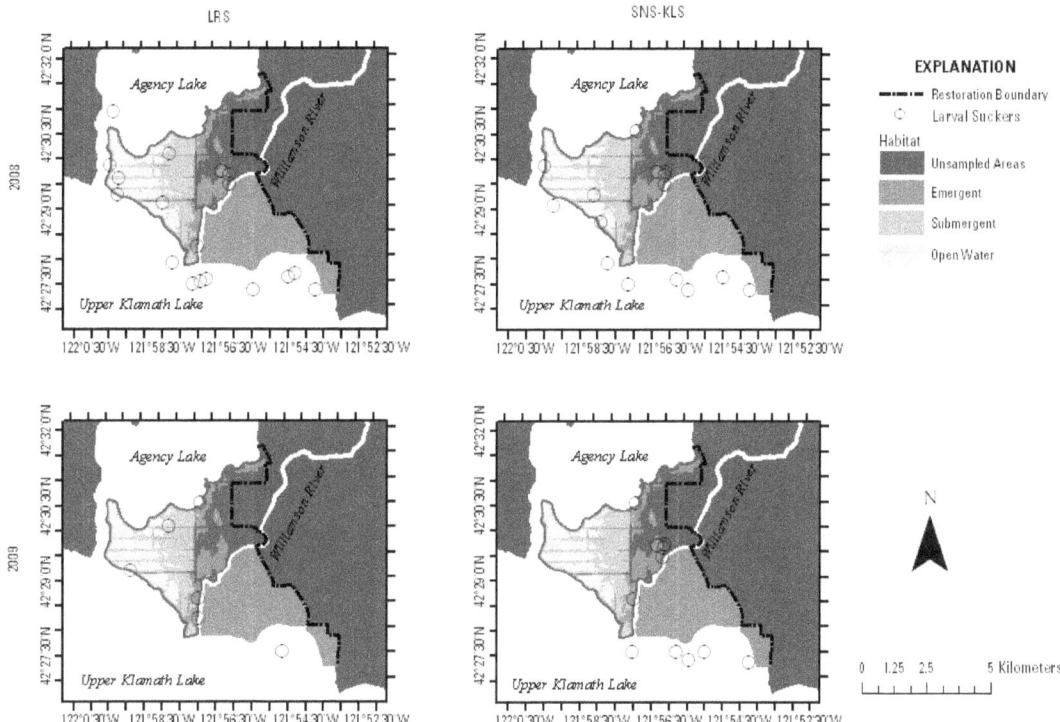

Figure 5. Locations where larval Lost River suckers (LRS) and larvae identified as either shortnose or Klamath largescale suckers (SNS-KLS) were captured in Agency Lake, Upper Klamath Lake, and the Williamson River Delta Preserve, Oregon, 2008–09. Sampling for larval suckers did not occur in Goose Bay or South Marsh habitats, located to the southeast of the Williamson River.

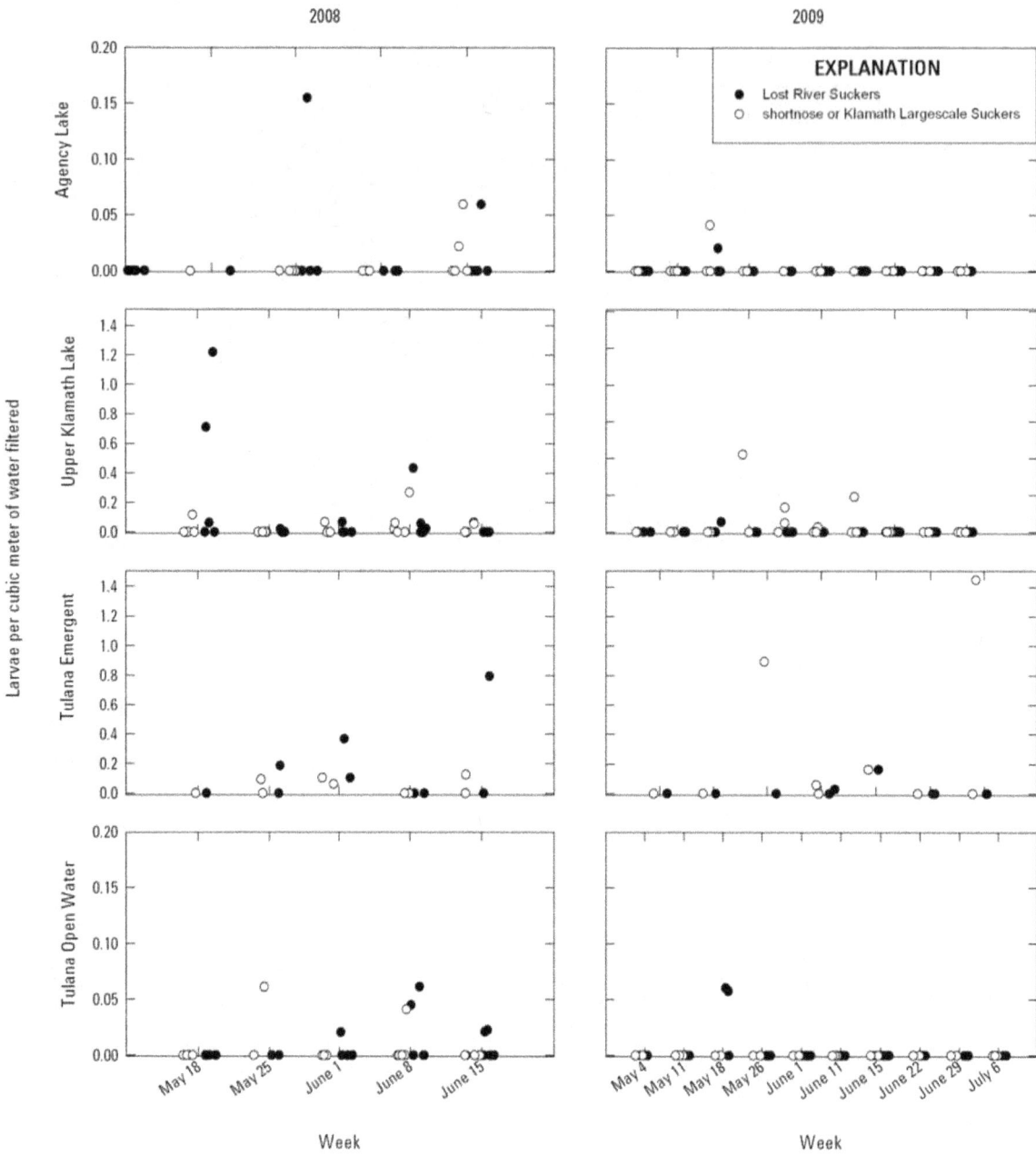

Figure 6. Number of larval Lost River and shortnose or Klamath largescale suckers caught per cubic meter of water filtered, by week in 2008 and 2009, in two habitats in the Williamson River Delta Preserve (Tulana Emergent and Tulana Open Water), in Upper Klamath Lake, and in Agency Lake, Oregon.

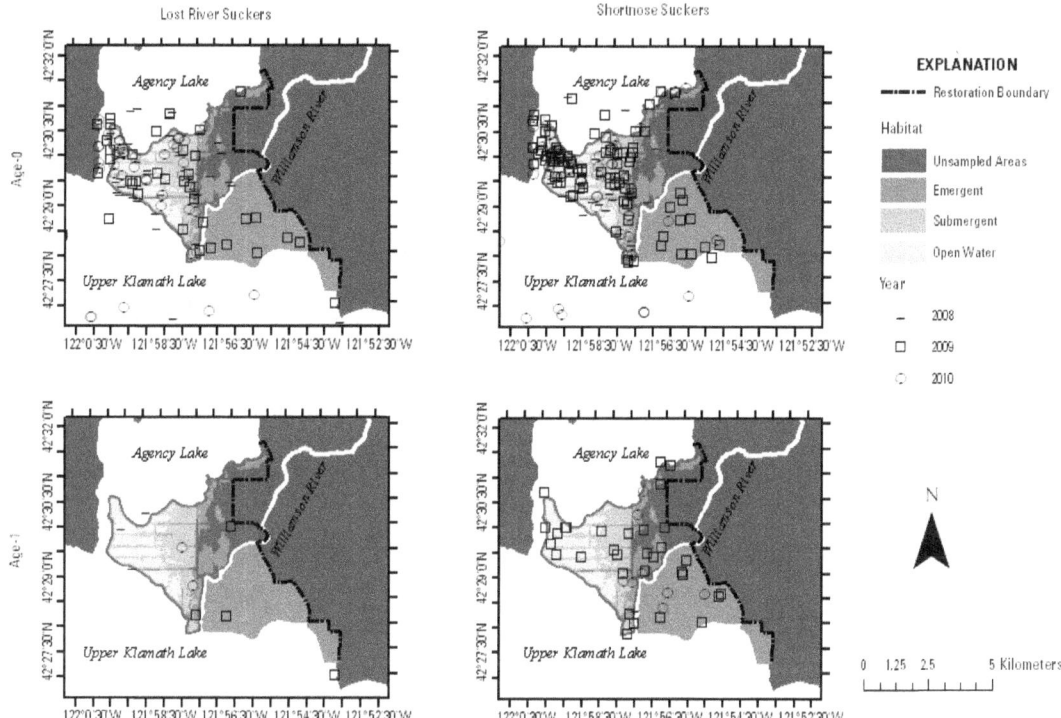

Figure 7. Locations that age-0 and age-1 Lost River suckers and shortnose suckers were captured in trap-net sampling in the Williamson River Delta, Oregon, and adjacent lake habitats, 2008–10.

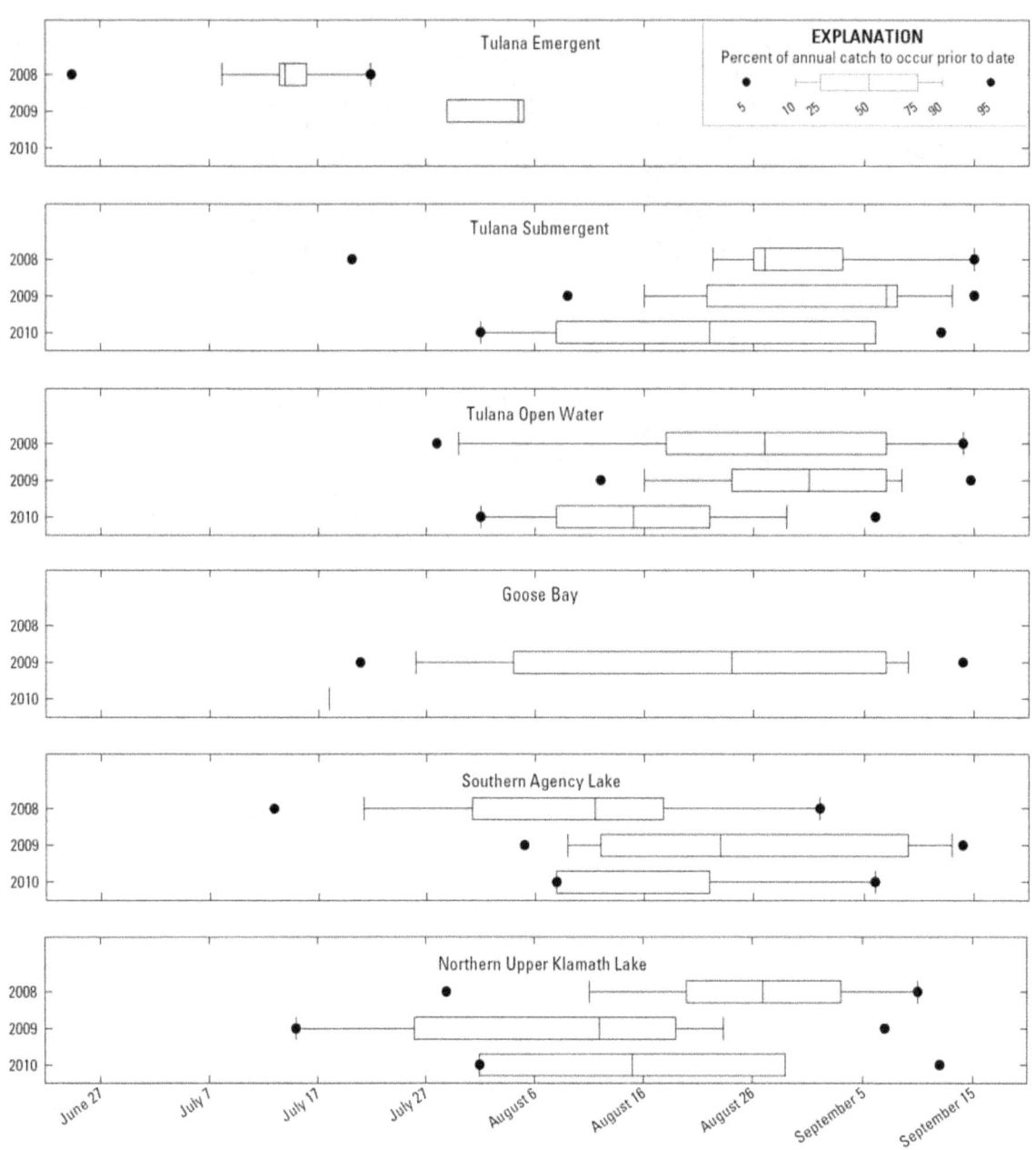

Figure 8. Schematic boxplots showing timing of age-0 sucker catches in trap nets set in four habitats in the Williamson River Delta Preserve and in northern Upper Klamath Lake, and in southern Agency Lake, Oregon, 2008–10. The Goose Bay habitat was not inundated in 2008 and therefore not sampled. The absence of data in the Tulana Emergent habitat in 2010, however, is due to a lack of age-0 suckers captured there in that year.

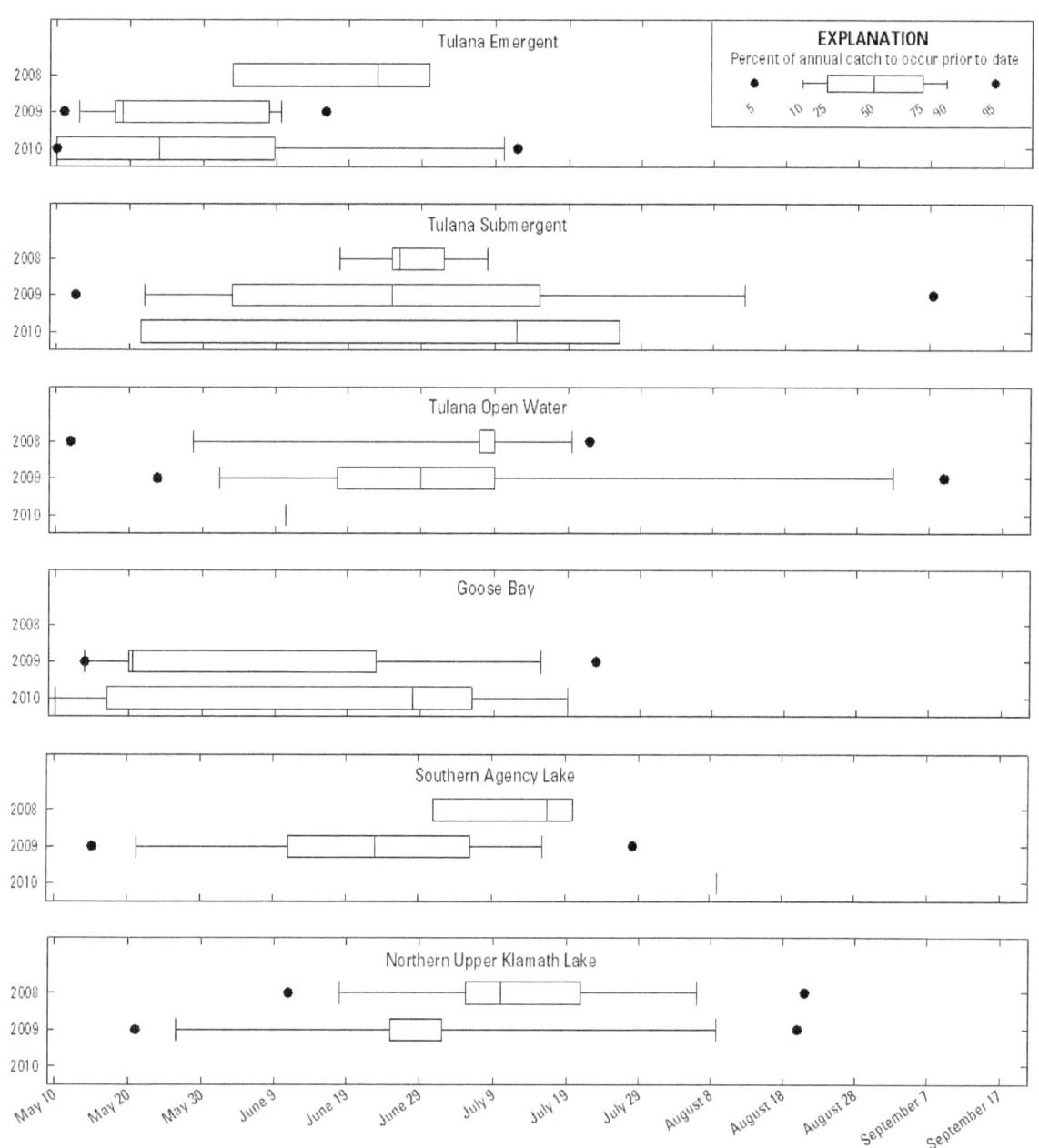

Figure 9. Schematic boxplots showing timing of age-1 sucker catches in trap nets set in four habitats in the Williamson River Delta Preserve and in northern Upper Klamath Lake, and in southern Agency Lake, Oregon, 2008–10. The Goose Bay habitat was not inundated in 2008 and therefore not sampled. The absence of data in northern Upper Klamath Lake in 2010, however, is due to a lack of age-1 suckers captured there in that year.

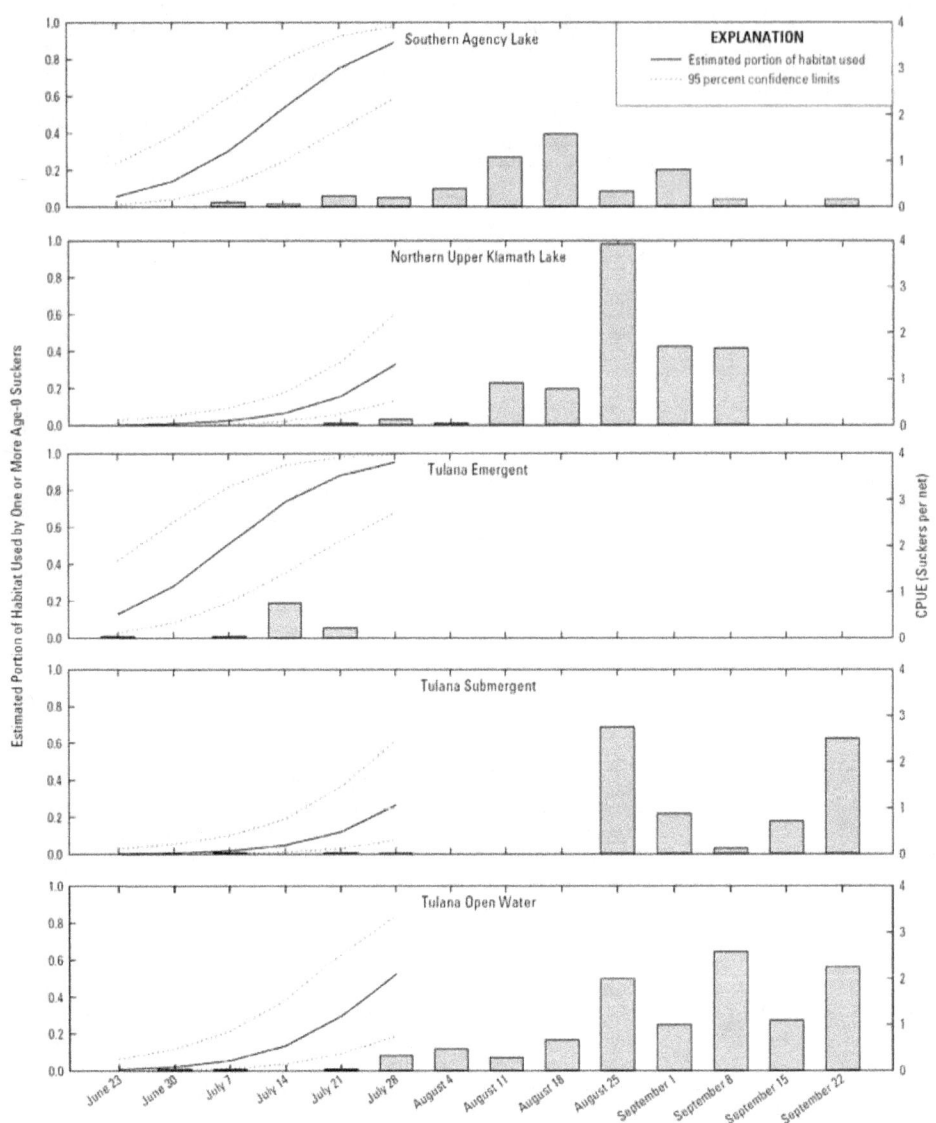

Figure 10. Estimated portion of habitat used by age-0 juvenile suckers in the Williamson River Delta Preserve and two adjacent lake habitats, Oregon, over time in 2008. Estimates are based on model averaging. Gray bars indicate the number of age-0 suckers captured per net set in each week. The portion of used habitat is an estimate in which imperfect detection has been accounted for. Therefore, all habitat can be in use when catch rates are fewer than one fish per net. The location of habitats is shown in figure 2.

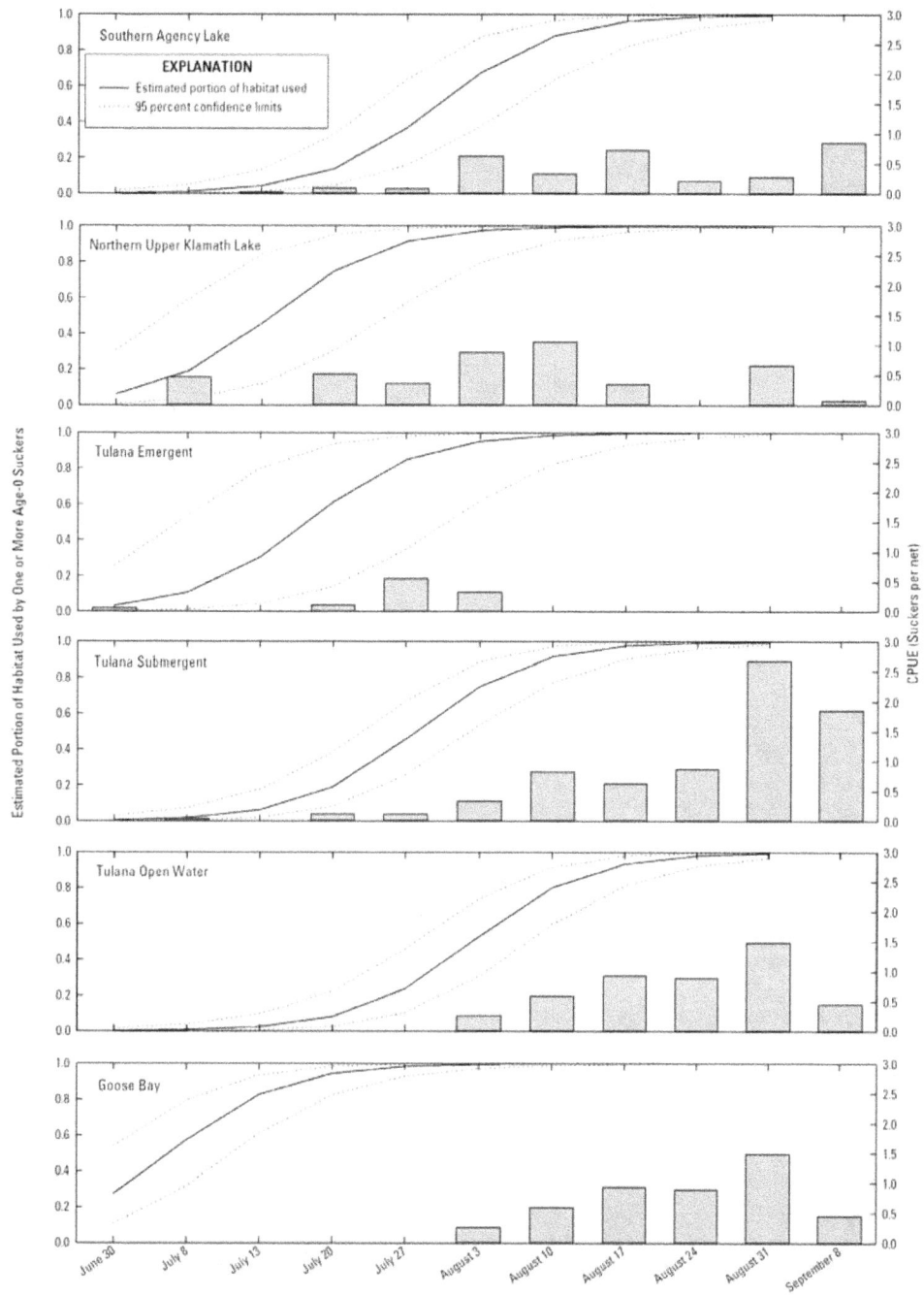

Figure 11. Estimated portion of habitat used by age-0 juvenile suckers in the Williamson River Delta Preserve and two adjacent lake habitats, Oregon, over time in 2009. Estimates are based on model averaging. Gray bars indicate the number of age-0 suckers captured per net set in each week. The portion of used habitat is an estimate in which imperfect detection has been accounted for. Therefore, all habitat can be in use when catch rates are fewer than one fish per net. The location of habitats is shown in figure 2.

35

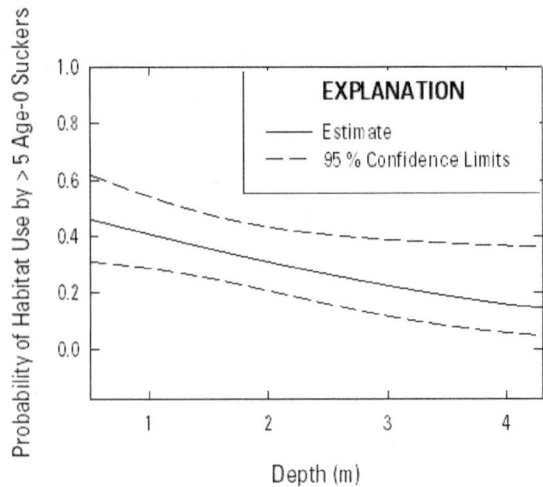

Figure 12. Estimated probability that a sample site in Upper Klamath Lake, Agency Lake, or the Williamson River Delta, Oregon, was used in 2010 by more than five age-0 suckers at a given depth. Probability was estimated using a multistate occupancy model in which the probability that each site is used by at least one to five age-0 suckers was fixed at one. 95-percent confidence limits are shown.

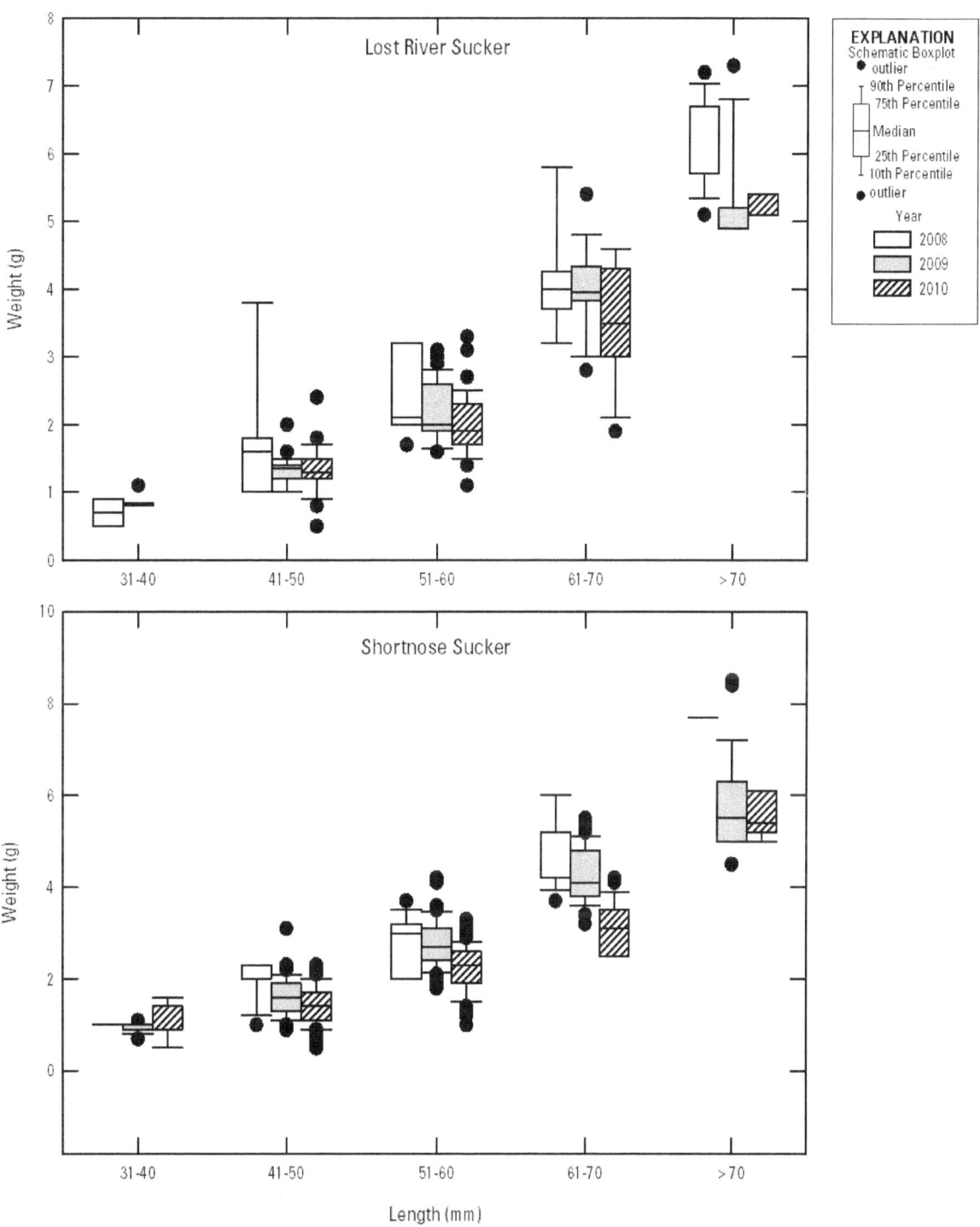

Figure 13. Schematic box plots showing age-0 Lost River and shortnose sucker weight in 10 mm length bins, captured in Agency Lake, Upper Klamath Lake, and the Williamson River Delta, Oregon, 2008–10.

Table 1. Number of fish species, excluding endangered suckers, captured in trap nets each year in six habitats sampled in and adjacent to the Williamson River Delta, Oregon.

[Goose Bay was dry and therefore not sampled in 2008 and data were not collected on fishes other than suckers in southern Agency Lake in 2010. A species list is given in table 2. --, no data]

Habitat	Number of species detected			
	2008	2009	2010	Total
Southern Agency Lake	11	13	--	13
Northern Upper Klamath Lake	12	13	10	13
Tulana Emergent	10	12	11	13
Tulana Submergent	12	12	10	13
Tulana Open Water	11	10	10	11
Goose Bay	--	13	10	14

Table 2. Characteristics of fishes, excluding endangered suckers, captured in and adjacent to the Williamson River Delta, Oregon.

[Fish were captured in trap nets or larval trawls. Life stages detected: A, adult, J, juvenile, and L, larval. Abundance: A qualitative classification based on the number of fish captured. Sucker life stage at risk of predation: An assumption based on diet and feeding behavior reported in the literature for each species. TL: total length. mm: millimeter]

Common name	Latin name	Native or non-native	Life Stages Detected	Abundance	Diet	Sucker life stage at risk of predation
blue chub	*Gila coerulea*	Native	A,J,L	Abundant	Algae, detritus, invertebrates, and fish (Bond and others, 1968)	Larval
brown bullhead	*Ameiurus nebulosus*	Non-native	A,J,L	Common	Invertebrates (Kline and Wood, 1996)	None
fathead minnow	*Pimephales promelas*	Non-native	A,J,L	Abundant	Algae, invertebrates, zooplankton, detritus, larval suckers (Markle and Dunsmoor, 2007)	Larval
Klamath Lake sculpin	*Cottus princeps*	Native	A,J[1]	Common	Invertebrates (Bond and others, 1968)	None
Klamath largescale sucker	*Catostomus snyderi*	Native	J,L	Very rare	Probably invertebrates (Markle and Clauson, 2006)	None
Klamath redband trout	*Oncorhynchus mykiss subsp.*	Native	J	Rare	Invertebrates and fish (Bond and others, 1968)	Larval and juvenile
Klamath speckled dace	*Rhinichthys osculus klamathensis*	Native	A	Very rare	Invertebrates (Angradi and others, 1991)	None
Klamath tui chub	*Siphatales bicolor bicolor*	Native	A,J,L	Abundant	Algae, detritus, and invertebrates (Bond and others, 1968, Koch, 1973)	Larval[2] and egg
largemouth bass	*Micropterus salmoides*	Non-native	J	Very rare	Invertebrates and fish (Dibble and Harrell, 1997)	Larval and juvenile suckers up to about 150 mm TL (Johnson and Post, 1996)
Sunfish (bluegill or pumpkinseed)	*Lepomis sp.*	Non-native	A,J	Rare	Invertebrates and fish (Garcia-Berthou and Moreno-Amich, 2000)	Larval
slender sculpin	*Cottus tenuis*	Native	A,J[1]	Rare	Invertebrates (Bond and others, 1968)	None
unidentified species of lamprey	*Lampetra sp.*	Native	A	Rare	Parasitic (Beamish, 1980)	Juvenile and adult
Upper Klamath marbled sculpin	*Cottus klamathensis klamathensis*	Native	A,J[1]	Abundant	Invertebrates (Bond and others, 1968)	None
yellow perch	*Perca flavescens*	Non-Native	A,J,L	Abundant	Invertebrates and fish (Bond and others, 1968)	Larval and juvenile suckers up to about 121 mm TL (Truemper and Lauer, 2005)

[1]Larval and juvenile sculpin were only identified to genus.

[2]Bond and others (1968) found fish in the diets of blue chub but not tui chub collected from Upper Klamath Lake. Koch 1973 reported that tui chub ate cui-ui sucker eggs.

Table 3. Ratio of the number of juvenile or small adult fish that potentially prey on larval suckers to those that do not prey on larval suckers, captured in and adjacent to the Williamson River Delta, Oregon, 2008–10.

[Locations of these areas are shown in figure 2. --, no data]

Habitat	2008	2009	2010
Tulana Emergent	23	30	110
Tulana Submergent	51	216	69
Tulana Open Water	60	441	49
Goose Bay	--	60	35
Southern Agency Lake	28	141	--
Northern Upper Klamath Lake	9	23	22

Table 4. Ratio of the number of juvenile or small adult fish that potentially prey on age-0 juvenile suckers to those that do not prey on age-0 juvenile suckers, captured in and adjacent to the Williamson River Delta, Oregon, 2008–10.

[Locations of these areas are shown in figure 2. –, no data]

Habitat	2008	2009	2010
Tulana Emergent	0.13	0.06	0.01
Tulana Submergent	0.10	0.01	0.03
Tulana Open Water	0.15	0.01	0.15
Goose Bay	--	0.21	0.01
Southern Agency Lake	0.15	0.00	--
Northern Upper Klamath Lake	0.16	0.02	0.03

Table 5. Ratio of the number of native fish to non-native fish, captured in and adjacent to the Williamson River Delta, Oregon, 2008–10.

[Locations of these areas are shown in figure 2. –, no data]

Habitat	2008	2009	2010
Tulana Emergent	1.33	0.87	1.54
Tulana Submergent	0.75	0.08	0.66
Tulana Open Water	0.61	0.08	0.52
Goose Bay	--	0.37	1.10
Southern Agency Lake	1.36	0.08	--
Northern Upper Klamath Lake	1.45	0.63	1.60

Table 6. Percentage of nets set in and adjacent to the Williamson River Delta that captured Lost River sucker larvae and larvae identified as either shortnose or Klamath largescale sucker, Oregon, 2008–09.

[Locations of these areas are shown in figure 2]

Area	2008		2009	
	SNS-KLS	LRS	SNS-KLS	LRS
Agency Lake	5	5	5	5
Upper Klamath Lake	14	16	19	4
Tulana Open Water	4	10	0	9
Tulana Emergent	50	50	63	25

Table 7. Ratio of larvae identified as Lost River suckers to those identified as either shortnose or Klamath largescale suckers collected in four sampling areas in and adjacent to the Williamson River Delta, Oregon, 2008–09.

[Locations of these areas are shown in figure 2]

Area	2008	2009
Agency Lake	1.50	0.50
Upper Klamath Lake	5.86	0.05
Tulana Open Water	2.00	no SNS-KLS
Tulana Emergent	3.83	0.02

Table 8. Ratio of age-0 juvenile Lost River suckers to shortnose suckers collected in six sampling areas in and adjacent to the Williamson River Delta, Oregon, 2008–10.

[Northern Upper Klamath Lake and southern Agency Lake were not divided into smaller sampling units in 2008 and 2009. Therefore, to facilitate comparisons the 2010 Fish Banks and Mid-North habitats were combined under the heading of northern Upper Klamath Lake and the 2010 Agency Near Shore and Agency Strait were combined under the heading of southern Agency Lake. Sampling areas are shown in figures 2 and 3]

Area	2008	2009	2010
Southern Agency Lake	2.43	0.15	1.80
Northern Upper Klamath Lake	0.42	1.68	0.46
Tulana Open Water	0.23	0.20	0.29
Tulana Submergent	0.28	0.11	0.40
Tulana Emergent	5.25	1.00	no suckers
Goose Bay	dry	0.53	all SNS

Table 9. Number of age-0 suckers caught per net set in each of six areas in and adjacent to the Williamson River Delta, Oregon, 2008–10.

[Northern Upper Klamath Lake and southern Agency Lake were not divided into smaller sampling units in 2008 and 2009. Therefore, to facilitate comparisons, the 2010 Fish Banks and Mid-North habitats were combined under the heading of northern Upper Klamath Lake, and the 2010 Agency Near Shore and Agency Strait were combined under the heading of southern Agency Lake. Sampling areas are shown in figures 2 and 3. --, no data]

Area	2008	2009	2010
Southern Agency Lake	0.263	0.183	0.587
Northern Upper Klamath Lake	0.257	0.192	1.016
Tulana Emergent	0.177	0.042	0.000
Tulana Open Water	0.489	0.331	0.917
Tulana Submergent	0.245	0.427	0.425
Goose Bay	--	0.644	0.025

Table 10. Number of age-1 suckers caught per net set in each of six areas in and adjacent to the Williamson River Delta, Oregon, 2008–10.

[Northern Upper Klamath Lake and southern Agency Lake were not divided into smaller sampling units in 2008 and 2009. Therefore, to facilitate comparisons, the 2010 Fish Banks and Mid-North areas were combined under the heading of northern Upper Klamath Lake, and the 2010 Agency Near Shore and Agency Strait areas were combined under the heading of southern Agency Lake. Sampling areas are shown in figures 2 and 3. , no data]

Area	2008	2009	2010
Southern Agency Lake	0.015	0.055	0.005
Northern Upper Klamath Lake	0.031	0.053	0.000
Tulana Emergent	0.025	0.352	0.067
Tulana Open Water	0.087	0.070	0.003
Tulana Submergent	0.045	0.080	0.008
Goose Bay	--	0.287	0.045

Table 11. Models fit to age-0 sucker habitat use data collected the Williamson River Delta, Oregon, and adjacent lake habitats, 2008.

[Each model is a mathematical description of a working hypothesis about the effects of covariates on habitat use (ψ) and detection probability (p). Habitats included: southern Agency Lake, northern Upper Klamath Lake, Tulana Emergent, Tulana Submergent, and Tulana Open Water (fig. 2). Covariate effects are listed after each parameter in the model name. A dot indicates no covariate effects were tested for a particular parameter within a model. Akaike's Information Criteria adjusted for small sample size is given (AICc) along with the difference in this value between the most parsimonious model and the given model (Delta AICc). Model weights are the probability that a given model is the most parsimonious model in the set to explain the data]

Model	Number of parameters	AICc	DeltaAICc	Weight
p(.)Ψ (habitat + week)	7	318.5	0	0.43
p(week) Ψ (habitat + week)	8	319.0	0.5	0.34
p(depth) Ψ (habitat + week)	8	320.6	2.1	0.15
p(habitat)Ψ(habitat + week)	11	322.0	3.5	0.08
p(habitat)Ψ(week)	7	326.3	7.8	0.01
p(week)Ψ(.)	3	340.1	21.6	0.00
p(week)Ψ(depth)	4	341.8	23.3	0.00
p(.)Ψ(week)	3	341.9	23.3	0.00
p(week)Ψ(week)	4	342.1	23.6	0.00
p(depth)Ψ(week)	4	343.1	24.6	0.00
p(.)Ψ(habitat)	6	346.3	27.8	0.00
p(depth)Ψ(habitat)	7	348.3	29.8	0.00
p(habitat)Ψ(.)	6	352.0	33.5	0.00
p(habitat)Ψ(depth)	7	354.1	35.5	0.00
p(.)Ψ(.)	2	360.5	42.0	0.00
p(depth)Ψ(.)	3	360.8	42.2	0.00
p(.)Ψ(depth)	3	361.3	42.8	0.00
p(depth)Ψ(depth)	4	362.8	44.3	0.00

Table 12. Models fit to age-0 sucker habitat use data collected the Williamson River Delta, Oregon, and adjacent lake habitats, 2009.

[Each model is a mathematical description of a working hypothesis about the effects of covariates on habitat use (ψ) and detection probability (p). Habitats included: southern Agency Lake, northern Upper Klamath Lake, Tulana Emergent, Tulana Submergent, Tulana Open Water, and Goose Bay (fig. 2). Covariate effects are listed after each parameter in the model name. A dot indicates no covariate effects were tested for a particular parameter within a model. Akaike's Information Criteria adjusted for small sample size is given (AICc) along with the difference in this value between the most parsimonious model and the given model (Delta AICc). Model weights are the probability that a given model is the most parsimonious model in the set to explain the data]

Model	Number of parameters	AICc	DeltaAICc	Weight
p(depth)Ψ(habitat + week)	9	1,155.8	0	0.99
p(.)Ψ(habitat + week)	8	1,166.7	10.9	0.00
p(week)Ψ(habitat + week)	9	1,166.8	11.0	0.00
p(habitat)Ψ(week)	8	1,179.2	23.4	0.00
p(depth)Ψ(week)	4	1,193.9	38.0	0.00
p(.)Ψ(week)	3	1,204.6	48.8	0.00
p(week)Ψ(week)	4	1,206.3	50.4	0.00
p(week)Ψ(depth)	4	1,247.6	91.8	0.00
p(week)Ψ(.)	3	1,256.8	101.0	0.00
p(habitat)Ψ(depth)	8	1,289.4	133.5	0.00
p(depth)Ψ(habitat)	8	1,301.0	145.1	0.00
p(depth)Ψ(depth)	4	1,301.9	146.0	0.00
p(.)Ψ(depth)	3	1,303.5	147.7	0.00
p(depth)Ψ(.)	3	1,306.6	150.7	0.00
p(habitat)Ψ(.)	7	1,306.7	150.8	0.00
p(habitat)Ψ(habitat)	12	1,310.1	154.3	0.00
p(.)Ψ(habitat)	7	1,311.5	155.6	0.00
p(.)Ψ(.)	2	1,321.4	165.6	0.00

Table 13. Explanatory habitat use models fit to age-0 sucker categorical abundance data collected from the Williamson River Delta, Oregon, and adjacent habitats, 2010.

[Models have parameters for low (1-5 age-0 suckers; Ψ_{low}) and high (> 5 age-0 suckers; Ψ_{high}) states of abundance, the probability of detecting each of these states (p_i), and the probability of observing a high abundance when a high abundance was present (δ). Parentheses after each parameter indicate covariates specific to that parameter. A dot indicates no covariates were applied to a parameter. Habitats included: Tulana Emergent, Tulana Submergent, Tulana Open Water, Agency Strait, Agency Near Shore, Fish Banks, and Mid North (figs. 2 and 3)]

Model
Ψ_{low} (.) Ψ_{high} (.) p_{low}(.)p_{high}(.)δ (.)
Ψ_{low} (habitat) Ψ_{high} (habitat) p_{low}(.)p_{high}(.)δ (.)
Ψ_{low} (depth) Ψ_{high} (habitat) p_{low}(.)p_{high}(.)δ (.)
Ψ_{low} (habitat+depth) Ψ_{high} (habitat) p_{low}(.)p_{high}(.)δ (.)
Ψ_{low} (.) Ψ_{high} (habitat) p_{low}(.)p_{high}(.)δ (.)
Ψ_{low} (habitat) Ψ_{high} (depth) p_{low}(.)p_{high}(.)δ (.)
Ψ_{low} (depth) Ψ_{high} (depth) p_{low}(.)p_{high}(.)δ (.)
Ψ_{low} (habitat+depth) Ψ_{high} (depth) p_{low}(.)p_{high}(.)δ (.)
Ψ_{low} (.) Ψ_{high} (depth) p_{low}(.)p_{high}(.)δ (.)
Ψ_{low} (habitat) Ψ_{high} (habitat+depth) p_{low}(.)p_{high}(.)δ (.)
Ψ_{low} (depth) Ψ_{high} (habitat+depth) p_{low}(.)p_{high}(.)δ (.)
Ψ_{low} (habitat+depth) Ψ_{high} (habitat+depth) p_{low}(.)p_{high}(.)δ (.)
Ψ_{low} (.) Ψ_{high} (habitat+depth) p_{low}(.)p_{high}(.)δ (.)
Ψ_{low} (habitat) Ψ_{high} (.) p_{low}(.)p_{high}(.)δ (.)
Ψ_{low} (depth) Ψ_{high} (.) p_{low}(.)p_{high}(.)δ (.)
Ψ_{low} (habitat+depth) Ψ_{high} (.) p_{low}(.)p_{high}(.)δ (.)

Table 14. The confidence set of models fit to age-0 sucker categorical abundance data collected in the Williamson River Delta, southern Agency Lake, and northern Upper Klamath Lake, Oregon, 2010.

[The probability of a model being the most accurate of the models fit to data from each week (w_i) is given. Only the most parsimonious models with w_is summing to at least 0.9 (the confidence set) are shown. Models had parameters for low (1-5 age-0 suckers; Ψ_{low}) and high (> 5 age-0 suckers; Ψ_{high}) states of occupancy, the probability of detecting each of these states (p_i), and the probability of observing a high abundance when a high abundance was present (δ). Parentheses after each parameter indicate covariates specific to that parameter. A dot indicates no covariates were applied to a parameter. If standard errors overlapped one, the upper estimation limit for Ψ_{low} the parameter was fixed at one and indicated by a one in the parentheses.]

Week	Most parsimonious models	w_i
2-Aug	Ψ_{low} (habitat) Ψ_{high} (depth) $p_{low}(.)p_{high}(.)\delta$ (.)	0.42
	Ψ_{low} (habitat) Ψ_{high} (.) $p_{low}(.)p_{high}(.)\delta$ (.)	0.21
	Ψ_{low} (habitat+depth) Ψ_{high} (depth) $p_{low}(.)p_{high}(.)\delta$ (.)	0.14
	Ψ_{low} (habitat+depth) Ψ_{high} (.) $p_{low}(.)p_{high}(.)\delta$ (.)	0.09
	Ψ_{low} (habitat) Ψ_{high} (habitat) $p_{low}(.)p_{high}(.)\delta$ (.)	0.08
9-Aug	Ψ_{low} (1)Ψ_{high} (habitat) $p_{low}(.)p_{high}(.)\delta$ (.)	0.79
	Ψ_{low} (1)Ψ_{high} (habitat+depth) $p_{low}(.)p_{high}(.)\delta$ (.)	0.21
16-Aug	Ψ_{low} (1)Ψ_{high} (habitat) $p_{low}(.)p_{high}(.)\delta$ (.)	0.71
	Ψ_{low} (1)Ψ_{high} (habitat+depth) $p_{low}(.)p_{high}(.)\delta$ (.)	0.15
	Ψ_{low} (1)Ψ_{high} (depth) $p_{low}(.)p_{high}(.)\delta$ (.)	0.11
23-Aug	Ψ_{low} (1)Ψ_{high} (habitat+depth) $p_{low}(.)p_{high}(.)\delta$ (.)	0.91
30-Aug	Ψ_{low} (.)Ψ_{high} (depth) $p_{low}(.)p_{high}(.)\delta$ (.)	0.64
	Ψ_{low} (depth)Ψ_{high} (depth) $p_{low}(.)p_{high}(.)\delta$ (.)	0.15
	Ψ_{low} (.)Ψ_{high} (habitat) $p_{low}(.)p_{high}(.)\delta$ (.)	0.12
6-Sep	Ψ_{low} (.)Ψ_{high} (.) $p_{low}(.)p_{high}(.)\delta$ (.)	0.42
	Ψ_{low} (depth)Ψ_{high} (.) $p_{low}(.)p_{high}(.)\delta$ (.)	0.27
	Ψ_{low} (.)Ψ_{high} (depth)$p_{low}(.)p_{high}(.)\delta$ (.)	0.13
	Ψ_{low} (depth)Ψ_{high} (depth)$p_{low}(.)p_{high}(.)\delta$ (.)	0.08
13-Sep	Ψ_{low} (1)Ψ_{high} (.)$p_{low}(.)p_{high}(.)\delta$ (.)	0.89
	Ψ_{low} (1)Ψ_{high} (habitat)$p_{low}(.)p_{high}(.)\delta$ (.)	0.09

Table 15. Estimated portion of habitats used each week in 2010 by at least one age-0 sucker (ψ_{low}).

[Model averaged estimated probabilities (ψ_{low}) and their standard errors (SE) are given. The confidence set of models (table 14) was used in model averages. If estimates were equal to the upper estimation limit of one ψ_{low} was fixed at one and the standard error was not estimated. These boundary estimates are marked with an asterisk. We refined our habitat stratification between 2009 and 2010, such that Fish Banks and Mid-North are within the former Upper Klamath Lake habitat and Agency Strait and Agency Near Shore are within former Agency Lake (figs. 2 and 3). --, no data]

Week	Fish Banks		Mid-North		Agency Strait		Agency Near Shore		Tulana Open Water		Tulana Submergent	
	Ψ_{low}	SE	Ψ_{low}	SE	Ψ_{low}	SE	Ψ_{low}	SE	Ψ_{low}	SE	Ψ_{low}	SE
Aug 02	0.97	0.13	0.62	0.22					0.97	0.10	0.29	0.14
Aug 09					1.00*	--	1.00*	--	1.00*	--	1.00*	--
Aug 16	1.00*	--	1.00*	--					1.00*	--	1.00*	--
Aug 23					1.00*	--	1.00*	--	1.00*	--	1.00*	--
Aug 30	0.90	0.08	0.91	0.07					0.91	0.06	0.91	0.07
Sep 06					0.83	0.12	0.83	0.12	0.83	0.12	0.83	0.12
Sep 13	1.00*	--	1.00*	--					1.00*	--	1.00*	--

Table 16. Estimated portion of habitats used each week in 2010 by more than five age-0 suckers (ψ_{high}).

[Model-averaged estimated probabilities (ψ_{high}) and their standard errors (SE) are given. If the model averaged estimate of ψ_{low} was at or near the upper estimation boundary of one (table 15) it was fixed at one, leaving only four models remaining in the set. The confidence set of models was used in model averages, and was defined as the most parsimonious models with weight summing to at least 0.9 (table 14). Standard errors could not be calculated if estimates in any of the models being used in averages were equal to the upper boundary of one or lower boundary of zero in any of the confidence set of models (Aug. 30). We refined our habitat stratification between 2009 and 2010, such that Fish Banks and Mid North are within the former Upper Klamath Lake habitat and Agency Strait and Agency Near Shore are within former Agency Lake (figs. 2 and 3). --, no data]

Week	Fish Banks		Mid North		Agency Strait		Agency Near Shore		Tulana Open Water		Tulana Submergent	
	Ψ_{high}	SE	Ψ_{high}	SE	Ψ_{high}	SE	Ψ_{high}	SE	Ψ_{high}	SE	Ψ_{high}	SE
Aug 02	0.24	0.10	0.24	0.10					0.24	0.10	0.24	0.10
Aug 09					0.10	0.11	0.14	0.09	1.00	--	0.11	0.11
Aug 16	0.81	0.29	0.07	0.18					0.75	0.24	0.33	0.20
Aug 23					0.54	0.25	0.00	--	1.00	--	1.00	--
Aug 30	0.17	--	0.04	--					0.04	--	0.06	0.07
Sep 06					0.03	0.03	0.03	0.03	0.03	0.03	0.03	0.03
Sep 13	0.58	0.64	0.45	0.06					0.49	0.65	0.45	0.64

Table 17. Percentage of juvenile suckers collected from Upper Klamath Lake, Agency Lake, and the Williamson River Delta, Oregon, 2008–10 to have one or more deformed opercula in each year.

Age class	2008	2009	2010
Age-0	6.7	9.0	7.0
Age-1	9.0	7.0	9.0

Appendix - List of Products

List of products produced under or in association with Interagency Agreement 07AA200135 with the Bureau of Reclamation.

Journal Articles

Burdick, S.M., 2011, Tag loss and short-term mortality associated with passive integrated transponder (PIT) tagging of juvenile Lost River suckers: North American Journal of Fisheries Management, v. 31, p. 1,088–1,092.

Robertson, L.S., Ottinger, C.A., Burdick, S.M., and VanderKooi, S.P., *in press*, Development of a quantitative assay to measure expression of transforming growth factor β1 (TGF-β) in Lost River sucker (*Deltistes luxatus*) and shortnose sucker (*Chasmistes brevirostris*) and evaluation of potential pitfalls in use with field-collected samples: Journal of Fish and Shellfish Immunology.

Wood, T.M., Hendrixson, H.A., Markle, D., Erdman, C., Burdick, S.M., and Ellsworth, C., *in review*, Validation of a model to simulate larval sucker transport and retention in a recently restored river delta, Upper Klamath Lake, Oregon: Ecological Applications.

Peer Reviewed Reports

Burdick, S.M, 2012, Distribution and condition of larval and juvenile Lost River and shortnose suckers in the Williamson River Delta restoration project and Upper Klamath Lake, Oregon—2010 annual data summary: U.S. Geological Survey Open-File Report 2012-1027, 39 p. (Also available at http://pubs.usgs.gov/of/2012/1027/.)

Burdick, S.M., and Brown, D.T., 2010, Distribution and condition of larval and juvenile Lost River and shortnose suckers in the Williamson River Delta Restoration Project and Upper Klamath Lake, Oregon—2009 Annual Data Summary: U.S. Geological Survey Open-File Report 2010-1216, 78 p. (Also available at http://pubs.usgs.gov/of/2010/1216/.)

Burdick, S.M., Ottinger, C., Brown, D.T., VanderKooi, S.P., Robertson, L., and Iwanowicz, D., 2009, Distribution, health, and development of larval and juvenile Lost River and shortnose suckers in the Williamson River Delta restoration project and Upper Klamath Lake, Oregon—2008 annual data summary: U.S. Geological Survey Open-File Report 2009-1287, 76 p. (Also available at http://pubs.usgs.gov/of/2009/1287/.)

Wood, T.M., Hendrixson, H.A., Markle, D.F., Erdman, C.S., Burdick, S.M., Ellsworth, C.M., and Buccola, N.L., 2011, Dispersal of larval suckers at the Williamson River Delta, Upper Klamath Lake, Oregon, 2006-09: U.S. Geological Survey Scientific Investigations Report 2012-5016, 28 p. (Also available at *http://pubs.usgs.gov/sir/2012/5016/.*)

Fact Sheet

VanderKooi, S.P., Burdick, S.M., Echols, K.R., Ottinger, C.A., Rosen, B.H., and Wood, T.M., 2010, Algal toxins in Upper Klamath Lake, Oregon—Linking water quality to juvenile sucker health: U.S. Geological Survey Fact Sheet 2009-3111, 2 p. (Also available at http://pubs.usgs.gov/fs/2009/3111/.)

Presentations

Bottcher, J., and Burdick, S.M., 2011, Distribution of age-1 suckers relative to dissolved-oxygen in Upper Klamath Lake, Oregon: American Fisheries Society Annual Meeting, Platform Presentation, Seattle, Washington, March 7, 2011.

Bottcher, J., and Burdick S.M., 2011, Distribution of age-1 suckers relative to dissolved-oxygen in Upper Klamath Lake, Oregon: Pacific Northwest Science Conference, Platform Presentation, Vancouver, Washington, March 2, 2011.

Burdick, S.M., 2009, Ecology of juvenile lake suckers in Upper Klamath Lake, Oregon: Invited Platform Presentation, Upper Klamath Lake Cyanotoxin Working Group, Seattle, Washington, December 7, 2009.

Burdick, S.M., 2009, Estimating habitat use and distribution of two rare suckers in Upper Klamath Lake, Oregon: Invited Platform Presentation, Klamath Science Team, Sacramento, California, March 17, 2009.

Burdick, S.M. and D.T. Brown. 2009. Retention of larval endangered Lost River and shortnose suckers in the restored Williamson River Delta. Platform Presentation. United States Geological Survey Northwest Science Conference. Portland, Oregon. March 5 2009.

Burdick, S.M., and D. Hewitt. 2010. Can space replace time in occupancy studies when the method of detection requires retaining individuals? The American Fisheries Society Annual Meeting, Landscape and Fish Habitat Relationships Symposium, Platform Presentation. Pittsburgh, Pennsylvania. September, 16, 2010.

Burdick, S.M. 2010. Larval and Juvenile Sucker Studies in Upper Klamath Lake, Oregon. Briefing to the U.S. Bureau of Reclamation. Klamath Falls, Oregon. April 6, 2010.

Burdick, S.M. 2010. Lack of recruitment to spawning sucker populations and timing of juvenile sucker mortality in Upper Klamath Lake, Oregon. Invited Platform Presentation. Klamath Basin Science Conference. Medford, Oregon. February 3, 2010.

Burdick, S.M., N.P. Banish, E. Willy, and D.A. Hewitt. 2011. Distribution of the endemic slender sculpin relative to habitat variables within Upper Klamath Lake, Oregon. American Fisheries Society Annual Meeting, Platform Presentation. Seattle, Washington. September 7, 2011.

Carter, J.L., and Fend, S.V. 2009. Benthic invertebrates of Upper Klamath Lake, OR: The Chironomidae. Upper Klamath Lake Cyanotoxin Working Group. Seattle, Washington. December 7, 2009. Invited Platform Presentation.

Carter, J.L., and Fend, S.V. 2010. Within-year and among-year distributions of benthic invertebrates in Upper Klamath Lake and the newly restored delta wetlands: Klamath Basin Science Conference, February 1-5, 2010, Medford, Oregon. Invited Platform Presentation.

Densmore, C.L., C.A. Ottinger, K.R. Echols, T.M. Wood, S.P. VanderKooi, B.H. Rosen, and S.M. Burdick. 2010. Algal Toxins in Upper Klamath Lake, Oregon: Histopathology of age-0 Lost River and shortnose suckers in 2007 and 2008. Invited Platform Presentation. Klamath Basin Science Conference, Medford, OR, Feb 1-5.

Echols, K.R., T.M. Wood, C.A. Ottinger, B.H. Rosen, S.M. Burdick, and S.P. Vanderkooi. 2010. Cyanobacterial Toxins Found in Upper Klamath Lake, Oregon: Implications for Endangered Fish. Invited Platform Presentation. Klamath Basin Science Conference, Medford, OR, Feb 1-5.

Eldridge, S.L.C, K.E. Kannarr, T.M. Wood, K.R. Echols, B.H. Rosen, S.M. Burdick, C.A. Ottinger, and S.P. VanderKooi. 2010. Seasonal and Spatial Dynamics of Cyanobacteria and Associated Water Quality Variables in Upper Klamath Lake, Oregon. Invited Platform Presentation. Klamath Basin Science Conference, Medford, OR, Feb 1-5.

Erdman, C.S., T.M. Wood, H. Hendrixson, D.F. Markle, S.M. Burdick, and C. Ellsworth, 2012, Understanding the Impact of a Restored Delta in Upper Klamath Lake, Oregon on Larval Sucker Transport through the Use of a Hydrodynamic and Larval Transport Model. Oregon Chapter of the American Fisheries Society Annual Meeting, Platform Presentation, Eugene, Oregon, March 1, 2012.

Iwanowicz, D.D., C.A. Ottinger, K.R. Echols, T. Wood, S.P. VanderKooi, B.H. Rosen, and S.M. Burdick. 2010. Skin bacterial flora of age-0 Lost River and shortnose suckers in 2008: Nature Conservancy Delta Restoration Project and Upper Klamath Lake. Invited Platform Presentation. Klamath Basin Science Conference, Medford, OR, Feb 1-5.

Markle, D.F., T.M. Wood, N. Buccola, S.M. Burdick, C. Ellsworth, C. Erdman, H. Hendrixson. 2011. Modeling transport of larval suckers through a restored delta in Upper Klamath Lake, Oregon, using density-based and individual-based approaches. American Fisheries Society Larval Fish Conference, Platform Presentation. Wilmington, North Carolina. May 22, 2011.

Rosen, B.H. 2010. Direct and Indirect Consumption of Cyanobacteria by Juvenile Suckers in Klamath Lake, Oregon. Invited Platform Presentation. Klamath Basin Science Conference, Medford, OR, Feb. 1-5.

Rosen, B.H. 2010. Ecological Strategies Utilized by Cyanobacteria. Invited Platform Presentation. Klamath Basin Science Conference, Medford, OR, Feb 1-5.

VanderKooi, S.P., S.M. Burdick, and C.M. Ellsworth. 2009. The effects of habitat restoration on endangered fishes in the Upper Klamath Basin. Invited Platform Presentation. American Geophysical Union Fall Meeting. December 18, 2009.

VanderKooi, S.P. 2009. USGS fisheries research in the Klamath River Basin. Invited Presentation. Dept. of Interior Science Scoping Meeting: Klamath Network and Environs. Redding, CA. November 17, 2009.

VanderKooi, S.P. and C.A. Ottinger. 2009. Algal toxins and their effects on juvenile endangered Lost River and shortnose suckers in Upper Klamath Lake, Oregon. The American Fisheries Society Annual Meeting. Contributed Presentation. Contaminants and Toxicology Symposium. Nashville, TN. August 31, 2009.

VanderKooi, S.P. 2010. Biology and current status of Lost River and shortnose suckers. Invited Presentation. Klamath River Dam Removal – Resident Fish Expert Panel. Klamath Falls, OR. August 2, 2010.

Wood, T.M., Markle, D.F., T.M. Wood, N. Buccola, S.M. Burdick, C. Ellsworth, C. Erdman, H. Hendrixson. 2011. Modeling transport of larval suckers through a restored delta in Upper Klamath Lake, Oregon, using density-based and individual-based approaches. American Fisheries Society Annual Meeting, Platform Presentation. Seattle, Washington. September 7, 2011.

Wood, T., and S.M. Burdick. 2009. The effects of hydrodynamics on larval sucker distribution in the Williamson River Delta restoration area, Oregon. Invited Platform Presentation. Klamath Science Team. Sacramento, California. March 17 2009.

Posters

Burdick, S.M., Wahrenbrock, D. and Bottcher, J. 2011. Readability of daily increments on sagittal and lapilliar otoliths of wild Lost River, shortnose and Klamath largescale sucker larvae. Pacific Northwest Science Conference. Vancouver, Washington, March 3, 2011.

Brown, D., S. Wong, S. Burdick, and H. Hendrixson. 2010. Effects of Low Dissolved Oxygen Concentration on the Distribution of Juvenile Suckers within the Williamson River Delta, Upper Klamath Lake, Oregon. Klamath Basin Science Conference. Medford, Oregon, February 3 2010.

Bottcher, J., and S. Burdick. 2010. Age-1 Lost River and Shortnose Sucker Distribution, Habitat Use, and Apparent Movement in Upper Klamath Lake, Oregon. Klamath Basin Science Conference. Medford, Oregon, February 3 2010.

Hendrixson, H.A., T. M. Wood, C. Erdman, C. Ellsworth, S. Burdick, D. Markle, N.L. Buccola. 2010. Modeling larval sucker transport through the Williamson River Delta, Upper Klamath Lake, Oregon. Klamath Basin Science Conference. Medford, Oregon, February 3 2010.